COOKING ON THE

Big
Green
Egg®

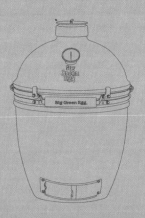

**EVERYTHING YOU NEED TO
KNOW FROM SET-UP TO
COOKING TECHNIQUES,
WITH 70 RECIPES**

JAMES WHETLOR

COOKING ON THE

Big Green Egg®

**EVERYTHING YOU NEED TO
KNOW FROM SET-UP TO
COOKING TECHNIQUES,
WITH 70 RECIPES**

JAMES WHETLOR

Photography by Sam Folan
Illustrations by Sarah Fisher

Hardie Grant

QUADRILLE

CONTENTS

Foreword by Tom Kerridge   6

Introduction   8

Lighting and Using Your EGG   12

Setting Up Your EGG   16

All in Pursuit of Flavour   24

    Fuel   26

    Tools and Equipment   30

    Ingredients   40

The First Recipe: Chicken Wings   46

Roast Chicken to Brisket   50

Grilling   76

Plancha   92

Dirty and Afterburners   102

Low and Slow   116

Roasting   136

Dutch Oven   152

Baking   168

Sauces and Condiments   180

Index   194

Endnotes   204

Acknowledgements   206

Suppliers   207

FOREWORD

Tom Kerridge

Best-selling cookbook author and chef patron at the extraordinary two Michelin-starred The Hand & Flowers pub in Marlow, UK.

Cooking on the Big Green Egg is an all-round experience: the warmth of the green dome, the aroma and crackle of the charcoal, the charring or gently smoking food inside. There's nothing else quite like it.

I love the whole process – getting outside, checking all the kit, lighting it up – all in anticipation of what's sure to be a brilliant meal at the end of the cooking. Once you've started, you know that inside there is a natural heat working to slow roast, or perhaps smoke, infusing your food with depths of flavour from the charcoal or wood smoke.

I've been using Big Green Eggs for years, both at home and for work – I have one at my pub, The Butcher's Tap, where we use it to cook amazing steaks, grilled chicken and fish, but are people who own one getting the most out of it? Now, at last – we have a book that can help us all get the most out of our Big Green Eggs.

I think James guessed, perhaps rightly, that a lot of Big Green Eggs sit out in people's gardens for most of the year unused, only to be fired up on those rare sunny summer days to cook the BBQ staples. And isn't that a shame? Isn't it sad that the great flavours you can achieve with an EGG are enjoyed only a few days a year? I feel hopeful that this book will inspire, and have you standing in the garden under an umbrella wearing a head torch before you know it. Why not use it in all weathers, and cook outside all year round? Once you've learned how to cook more favourites, and tried some recipes in this book, you'll be barbecuing in February, like I do!

This is set out to be more than just a cookbook. It will make you look at your Big Green Egg in a different light as it's not just a BBQ, it's more than that. I view it as an oven that just happens to live in the garden that can do all the things a conventional oven does, plus much more. There is nothing difficult about cooking on the EGG once you've got the hang of a few easy techniques, which are all laid out in this book. If you've ever wondered why the EGG is green, you will find your answer in this book. I wasn't expecting a brief Japanese history lesson when I opened the pages, but I got one! You'll learn a little about how to choose your charcoal, why it's worth investing in some decent tools, and why a quality piece of kit deserves quality ingredients. It's all pretty useful advice.

Now, I love my indoor cooking too. I've spent my entire career cooking with conventional ovens in various pubs and restaurants, but there are some things only a Big Green Egg can do. Think you make a decent curry? I am sure it's very tasty, but if you grill your meat first, then add it to the pot, you'll have added a whole other layer of charred tasty flavour.

The enthusiasm James has for cooking on the BGE is obvious, but so is his wish for you to enjoy it just as much as he does. These recipes break down the barriers between regular home cooks and those that cook on Big Green Eggs all the time. Cooking on the Big Green Egg will take you through all the BBQ classics, while helping you become a BBQ master. Plus, you will find some amazing recipes that you might never have considered cooking on your EGG. You might recognize a few, like the Paella on page 80, but cooking it on the EGG elevates and breathes new life into it.

The 12-step chicken to brisket chapter is genius. If you're like me, you'll want to cook those show-stopping dishes as soon as you can, but you can't do that without some basic knowledge. If you want to cook the perfect pulled pork or brisket, you have to do the hard work to learn the skills! What you will like about the 12-step plan is that you get to learn as you go in a simple, fun and delicious way. You'll be enjoying and learning to cook on your EGG straight away – cooking and eating your way to BBQ greatness.

For those of you who already live and breathe the BBQ life, there are loads of recipes in here for you too, with extra challenges to give you another excuse to fire up the EGG. Once you've nailed brisket and can bang out a great set of ribs, how about trying something a little more refined? You could have a go at the roast partridge (page 140), the whole roast turbot (page 78) or the duck breast (page 94). And if that's not your bag and you love the BBQ classics, there are some twists on staple recipes and techniques that you could try, too.

Big Green Eggs can become a way of life. I hope you'll occasionally commit to some long cooks – spend an hour prepping and then it's easy waiting a few hours more for the perfect, falling-off-the-bone finish to your meat. You'll need to invest in some kit and feed your new habit with charcoal but, trust me, it is worth it. The reward is in getting the absolute maximum out of the ingredients you cook.

Who doesn't want to be a BBQ force to be reckoned with? By the time you get through this book, I expect you'll be as confident with your EGG as you are at making cheese on toast!

INTRODUCTION

Ed Fisher, the man who gave Big Green Eggs to the world, didn't start out with a plan to sell BBQs. While visiting Japan, he had come across Pachinkos, a kind of vertical pinball machine, and on his return had started importing them into his store in a small shopping district of Atlanta. Business was good, the machines became popular arcade games among the teens of America, but it was seasonal: the Pachinkos sold well in the winter months, especially in the run-up to Christmas, but sales slowed in the summer. Mr Fisher was looking for something to even out the sales throughout the year.

He recalled a steak he'd been served during his visit to Japan that was cooked on an unusual-looking oven; the deliciousness of the steak and the theatre of the grill had stuck in his mind. He thought they might sell well in the BBQ-friendly southern USA and so started to import a few of the 'Kamados'. Sadly for Fisher, the combination of arcade game and foreign oven showroom didn't really work; he found that running adverts in the local press saying 'Kamado grill sold by Pachinko house' wasn't having the desired effect.

Then he had an idea... To improve his sales pitch and entertain his customers, he started cooking chicken wings on the Kamado ovens at the front of the store, letting the smoke carry down the street. And that was all it took. Soon sales picked up and the Pachinkos were forgotten, as the best chicken wings anyone had ever tasted gained the ovens a remarkable reputation.

There were problems, though. Not least the day he set up the Kamado outside his store as usual, chicken wings smoking, and someone backed up a truck, pushed the lot in and sped off! More significant than this minor setback, however, was the ovens' fragility – importing them from Japan, Taiwan and India was precarious. There were a lot of breakages in transit and Mr Fisher soon became fed up with sweeping the bits of broken clay and dust out of the containers. A further problem was that the imported ovens were liable to crack at high temperatures.

Mr Fisher decided he needed to take control of the design and manufacture of his own product, so in the mid-1990s he linked up with a ceramic manufacturing specialist in Mexico, which gave him the opportunity to tweak the design and incorporate better-quality materials. Thanks to NASA and the space shuttle programme developing ceramics and materials that could cope with extremely high temperatures, things

had moved on significantly. Soon the newly christened 'Big Green Eggs' were sporting this cutting-edge technology, and today every EGG sold anywhere in the world comes from the same factory. The process is mechanized, with thousands rolling out of the factory every year. A single 'matrix mould' is produced by hand, even the etching in of each dimple, with the ceramic slurry poured into moulds made from that one matrix. It is from that single matrix that the EGG comes, including the one sitting in your garden. The dimples themselves, which, other than its 'greenness', are perhaps the EGG's most distinguishing feature, fulfil two functions. Firstly, they make the EGGs easier to release from the mould and, secondly, they give a uniform finish which, if left smooth, would be difficult to achieve.

How did they come to be called 'Big Green Eggs'? Mr Fisher thought the name needed to be more memorable than 'Kamado' and, here, I wish I could convey a story as charming as the accident of cooking chicken wings, but I can't. They are called Big Green Eggs because they are big, shaped like eggs and Fisher liked the colour green. To him that simplicity seemed perfect. Success hasn't come from gimmicks or marketing; it has come because the EGGs are brilliant ovens that cook food so well that their owners tell all their friends about them.

Mr Fisher hasn't just put his stamp on the Big Green Eggs but on the world of cooking. BBQ is becoming a mainstream technique but the ovens they are based on – the Kamados – are old, very old, and have a fascinating story of their own. One where it's important to understand that Kamado probably isn't the right name for them.

The style of oven we know as Kamado is not unique to Japan. Similar kinds of oven made of earth or clay can be found everywhere. Tandoors, although synonymous with India, can be found all across Asia, with their close cousins tannours used in the Middle East. Hornos in South America are based on the southern Spanish clay ovens originally brought to Spain from Africa by the Moors, but huatia ovens are even older and pre-date the Conquistadors' invasion. Over time, this style of oven has evolved from being a pit in the ground with an overlay of earth or clay – these ovens are not standalone domes but built-in ovens, moulded into the dwelling. Not portable but fixed in position.

The word 'kamado', directly translated, means 'stove' or, more accurately, 'place for the stove', and is similar to 'hearth' in English, i.e. more than just an oven, a symbol of the home and family. Indeed, the Japanese have a saying: 'Kamado wo yaburu', which translates as 'break the stove', meaning to divide the family.

The development and use of Kamados in Japan ran on two separate paths. In the poor and rural kitchens, the focus until as recently as the 18th century was the 'irori', which functioned as both the cooking and emotional centre of the home, providing food, light and heat. It was little more than a pot suspended above an open fire, meaning meals were restricted to a perpetual one-pot stew. These kitchens have been described as miserable places, with the women – and it was only the women – having to squat to cook. The popularization of Kamados allowed the cooks to stand and – with the addition of a chimney – freed the kitchen of smoke, which must have improved life considerably.

The irori persisted in the northern parts of Japan, where the long, cold winters meant the homes required the heat. But fuel was a problem: historically, firewood has been both scarce and labour-intensive to generate in Japan. The country's two-and-a-half-century period of isolation from the rest of the world during the Tokugawa period (1603–1868) meant no trade and very little outside contact, alongside an economic expansion driven by farming and the growth of credit markets. This led to an increase in demand for timber for building, shipping and to produce charcoal for fuel, pressures that all fell on a finite and scarce resource and an inflation-dogged timber supply. The Kamados, with their enclosed and direct cooking, made them more efficient, and moving from an irori – which sat in the centre of a raised wooden living area – to a Kamado as the means of cooking changed the nature of living. Kamados were moved to a 'doma', an earth-floored area that was part-kitchen, part-utility room. This was a lot safer as it decreased the risk of fire, although there is some nostalgia today for the communal nature of the irori.

Wealthy and imperial households had Kamados much earlier, after they were introduced from Korea in the 4th century. Again, these Kamados were not the standalone ovens we are familiar with today, but more a cooking range akin to an Aga. They were designed to accommodate more than one pot, meaning rice could be cooked alongside other dishes, which had the side effect of improving the diets of the Japanese. They would be arranged across the north-facing wall, presumably because it was the coldest part of the kitchen, and also found industrial uses in salt-making and forging. The combination of fuel shortages, the growth of Kamado ovens, and urban development – with people living in small one- or two-room tenements – led to some families only cooking rice once a day and relying on small shops selling food for consumption at home, the Tokugawa period's fast-food industry...

The design of those early Kamados was quite simple. A raised clay dome gave space for the fire and there was an opening for the fuel. Suspended above that space and sticking out of the top of the clay dome was the 'kama', the iron pot that would hold the rice. The fire would boil the water, which in turn would heat the kama and cook the rice. However, controlling the heat, and therefore cooking the rice, using direct fire on the bottom of a metal bowl, was both difficult and time-consuming.

The innovation that led us to the Big Green Eggs was twofold. First came the 'Mushikamado', created in the early 20th century. These portable ovens were designed to cook rice in much the same way as the larger Kamados but, not being part of a cooking range, they were suitable for a smaller household. The second was the incorporation of the 'shichirin' into the Mushikamado – small, portable ceramic cookers about the size of a wastepaper basket. They became very popular because of the fuel economy they offered. The name is said to come from an amalgamation of the word for seven and the word 'rin', a coin used during the Tokugawa period and meaning it only cost seven rin to fill with charcoal. As the technology improved, vents were added at the bottom of the shichirin to regulate airflow, further improving its efficiency and versatility. This kind of oven is known in the West as a 'hibachi', which is a mistranslation, or misunderstanding (hibachis being small porcelain containers filled with lit charcoal, used as heaters).

By placing a slightly modified shichirin inside the Mushikamado and moving the air vents from the shichirin to the outer shell, an oven with controllable temperature and fuel consumption was achieved. It is not clear who first made this innovation, but it was probably designed to make cooking rice easier – cooking rice perfectly on a traditional Kamado is a tricky business. This new oven allowed the shutting off of the airflow on simmering rice, leaving the residual heat to cook it perfectly. Sadly for this technology, however, it was soon superseded when, in 1955, Toshiba launched the first commercially viable automatic electric rice cooker. Within the first year they were producing 200,000 a month, and by 1970 they reached 12.35 million a year. This revolutionized Japanese domestic kitchens and the lives of the women who occupied them, which is a fascinating story all of its own...

The Mushikamado with the shichirin inside became known in the US as 'hibachi pots' (thanks to that aforementioned mistranslation or misunderstanding); they may well have become obsolete had they not been exported to the US. Which brings us full circle, back to Mr Fisher. Seeing the hibachi pots as a grill and smoker, and seeing how they could be improved for the US market, led us to where we are today. Big Green Eggs are now sold in over 50 countries and have spawned a community of followers and enthusiasts around the world, inevitably known as 'Eggheads'.

Now well into his eighties, Mr Fisher is still chairman of the company, and his 'invention' marches on. Sadly, I haven't been able to track down the chicken wing recipe or rub he used back in the days of trying to coax more shoppers into the store, but as it was his first cook, I thought it was only right that I included my best interpretation of it in this book (page 46).

LIGHTING AND USING YOUR EGG

It looks complicated, doesn't it? And a little intimidating, this big hunk of ceramic in your back garden. The aim of the next few pages is to reassure you that, although it may look hard, setting up, lighting and cooking on the EGG is simple. So, let's start with lighting it.

Before the charcoal goes in, make sure the area underneath the fire box is clean. You want to allow the air intake through the bottom vent to flow with as little obstruction as possible. If you have coals left over from a previous cook, give them a stir to shake out all the ash. Once it's looking clean-ish (it's only ever going to look really clean once and that's the day you bought it) and ash-free, you're ready to load it with charcoal.

Fill the EGG with charcoal, pouring directly from the bag, halfway up the fire ring regardless of what or how you are cooking. This is important. Your EGG will burn more evenly and efficiently when filled with charcoal. If you are tipping new coals onto old ones, once you have filled the fire box, give it a stir so they are mixed together. You are now ready to light it.

Make sure the bottom vent is fully open. If you are using a firelighter, nestle one in the centre of the firebox – always use natural wood or sawdust lighters, never lighter fluid or chemical firelighters, which will taint the ceramics; you'll never get rid of the taste. Light it and leave it, keeping the lid open.

If you are using a blowtorch or fan lighter you won't need a firelighter. Just point the end at the centre of the EGG and press 'fire'. You are trying to create a core of heat and the coals should start to glow red and continue to do so when the firelight has burned out or when you remove the blowtorch or fan. This should take around 10 minutes with a firelighter and about 2 with a blowtorch or fan lighter.

Once this core is established, leave it. You are going to have to get used to not fiddling with your lit EGG, and this is a good first test. The temptation to give it a poke or a stir can be overwhelming but don't do it! The fire can now manage itself. If you do stir you will just burn though the charcoal much more quickly. This is not only less efficient but if you are going for a long cook it might burn out before you get your dinner. For now, the lid stays open.

Peering into your EGG after about 10 minutes, you should now see a nice even burn spreading out from the centre of your coals. Now is the time to close the lid. You have in mind your target temperature, which is to say, the temperature at which you want to start cooking your food. Preheating the oven is a concept we are all familiar with in conventional cooking, and when using your EGG, the principle is no different.

Your target temperature will vary depending on what you are cooking. It will be lower for low and slow cooking than for roasting or grilling, but you still want the whole EGG to be up to temperature before you start cooking. Again, this is about getting an even cook and burning the coals in the most efficient way. Each EGG has its own characteristics so there is no precise way of telling you where to set your bottom and top vents in order to get your target temperature. However, I suggest you start with both a quarter open to achieve 200°C / 400°F. Use this as your guide and adjust as required: narrow the vents for a lower temperature; open wider for a higher temperature. You want to come up slowly to your target so if the EGG really starts motoring towards 150°C / 300°F, ease both the vents to slightly less than a quarter open. This should slow it down. Keep in mind it is much easier to bring the temperature up on an EGG than to bring it down, and you will need to be patient and not fiddle too much – it will not respond as quickly as the dial on an electric cooker. Allow time for the adjustments you have made to take effect. If you want 200°C / 400°F and you have 210°C / 410°F, don't worry too much. The EGG is a very forgiving bit of kit, so don't sweat too much over 10–15 degrees either way.

Once you are at your target temperature, let it sit there for 15 minutes or so, just so you are sure it is where you need it to be. Now you can introduce, very carefully, the ceramics or cast iron you need for your cook.

A note here on opening a lit EGG. With an EGG, you are, obviously, cooking on live fire and that fire needs to be respected and treated with care. Once your EGG is burning it will be taking in oxygen through the bottom vent at a slow, even rate. This, in turn, makes the charcoal burn evenly. By lifting the lid you are introducing a sudden rush of oxygen. That rush can cause the coals to flare up. To avoid such a flare-up you should always 'burp' your EGG when opening it. Just lift the lid a little, no more than a few inches, let the oxygen in then let it drop back down. Ease it up and down slightly a few times more. Once that's done, you should then be fine to open it up fully. This is important at any stage, but you should take extra care when grilling food that will drip fat onto the lit coals below.

Introducing ceramics, cast irons or even a large cut of meat can sink your EGG's temperature by as much as 100°C/200°F. Any meat or fish that is in the fridge you should take out before you light your EGG, to bring it up to room temperature so it isn't added chilled, which would sink the temperature even more. Keep an eye on the thermometer. It will drop but soon start climbing again. You don't need to fiddle here. You have already set your vents to the correct temperatures.

Once it's up to temperature again you can add the veg, meat, fish or whatever it is you are cooking, and relax. The EGG will take care of the rest. The whole process, from adding the charcoal to closing the lid and opening a beer, should take about 30 minutes. EGGs will have you ready to cook in the same amount of time as a gas, pellet or traditional charcoal grill. Once it's chugging away the lid stays closed. The lid should always be closed when you are cooking – only ever lift it to add ceramics, turn what you are cooking or check your internal temperatures.

There will be recipes in this book that call for you to turn ingredients when browning or give something a stir. When you do this, burp the EGG, open the lid, do what you need to do and close it again. This may sound like a faff, but it's easy and you will get used to it, and it's essential practice. If you keep the EGG open for more than a few minutes you will start to lose control of the temperature.

If you are lighting your EGG, it makes sense to try to extend the cooking as much as possible. Just heating the ceramics takes a lot of energy, and good charcoal isn't cheap. To get the most out of each load, try to combine cooks. For example, light the EGG for a low and slow cook. Once that is done, increase the temperature and have something ready to grill, then when you shut the EGG down, throw in an afterburner. Three cooks from a single lighting. You don't have to do this, of course, but it's a nice thing to keep in mind.

Some of the recipes you are about to read will ask you to move bits of kit in and out of a hot EGG. Always take care when doing this. Have the right protective gloves and – my favourite cooking tip of all time – always know where you are going to put the hot thing down before you pick it up. Have a plan. It prevents a lot of swearing, a lot of panicking and a lot of breaking of things.

A quick note on accessories. There are hundreds of bits of kit you can buy to expand your EGG cooking options. In this book I have tried to keep their use to a minimum so everyone, regardless of what gear they own, can cook the recipes. The exceptions are the baking stone and the convEGGtor. I see these as essential parts of the EGG, and without them you will not fulfil its potential and will be missing out. They are worth the investment. The only other thing I would add to the list of essentials is a handheld digital probe thermometer. So much of the cooking you are about to do is about temperature not time. Generally, with EGG cooking, things are done when they reach the appropriate internal temperature, and you will only know what that is if you can stick a probe thermometer in it to check. It is indispensable.

If you ever feel like the temperature of your EGG is getting out of hand or flames are taking over slightly, don't worry. The Big Green Egg allows air flow to circulate efficiently, so all you need to do is close the lid and adjust the air flow systems using the vents. Temperature too high? Close both vents slightly. Temperature too low? Open both vents slightly. Soon you'll master complete control to within a few degrees! If you feel the flames are too big then step back. The flames will always be contained within the EGG. Close the bottom vent. Gently close the lid and then close the top vent. The fire, being starved of oxygen, will go out. Leave the EGG well alone until the thermometer says it's cool again. And I really shouldn't have to say this, but do not ever use the EGG for deep-frying. Heating cooking oil above a live fire is asking for trouble. Explosive, first-degree-burns kind of trouble.

Finally, for this book we tested all the recipes using a large Big Green Egg. Each size will cook a little differently so you may see some variation in the timings, depending on which size you have. In time you will get to know your EGG and these things will become second nature.

Now, let's have some fun...

SETTING UP YOUR EGG

The following pages show you the basic set-ups and bits of kit you'll need to cook every recipe in this book. Get to know your EGG in detail here, then follow the set-up instructions on each individual recipe.

CLOSED

OPEN

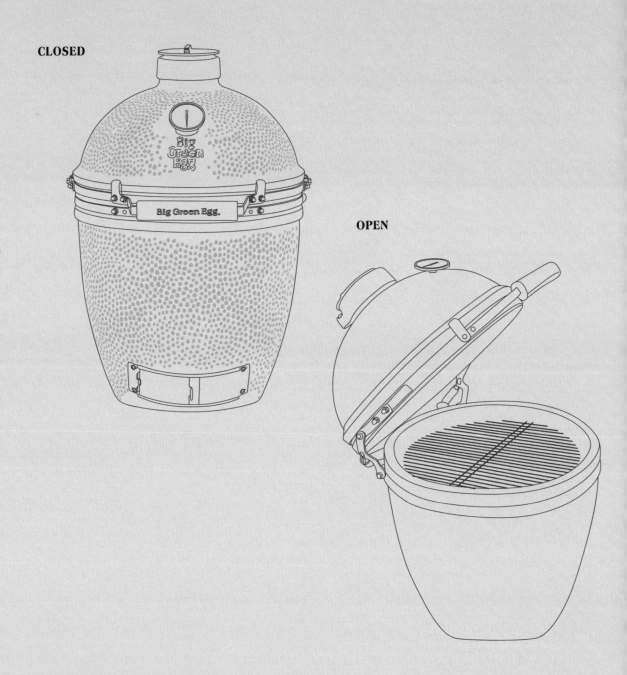

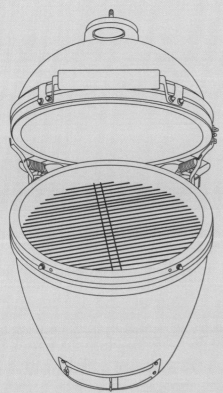

DIRECT SET-UP

What most people recognize as traditional BBQ-ing, in direct set-up the heat of the charcoal has direct contact with the food you are cooking. This means tasty, caramelized charlines and a distinct, smokey umami flavour. Test your skills with the recipes in the Grilling chapter on page 76.

INDIRECT SET-UP

Indirect set-up works like a convection oven. By blocking the fire's direct heat with a convEGGtor, you take away its intensity. This gives an even heat that deflects around the dome of the EGG. It provides the perfect cooking conditions for roasting (page 136), cooking low and slow (page 116) and smoking.

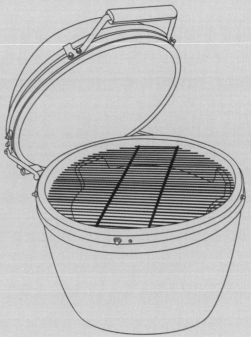

DIRTY

Cooking on your EGG in the most basic form allows the high-quailty lumpwood charcoal to give an intense, elemental flavour to your food.

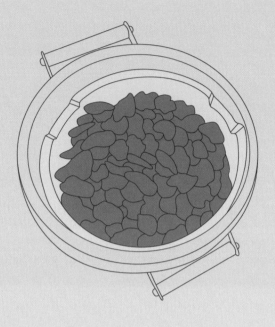

BAKING STONE (HALF)

To maximize on space, use the half moon baking stone to easily whip up some flatbreads while you're grilling the main event.

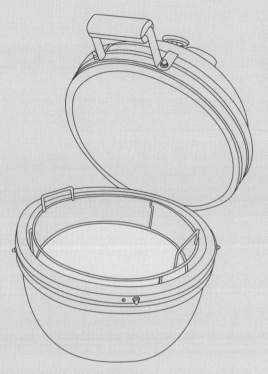

BAKING STONE (FULL)

Turn your EGG into a perfect pizza oven with the simple addition of a baking stone. Pulling moisture from the outer surface of the dough and distributing the heat evenly, you'll produce delicious breads and bakes.

CAST IRON GRID

For perfect sear marks and amazing heat retention, look no further than the cast iron grid.

DUTCH OVEN

Offering efficient heat distribution and excellent durability, the BGE cast iron Dutch oven is an essential addition to you BGE collection. A favourite for soups, stews and curries.

SKILLET

Searing, braising, baking, sautéing or roasting – the BGE cast iron skillet or paella pan is one of the most versatile pieces of kit you can own.

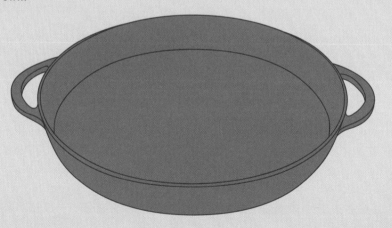

PLANCHA

With a dual-sided design, the BGE plancha is the perfect surface for sautéing vegetables, and for searing meat and fish. Authentic, high temperature grilling is made quick and easy with this great piece of kit.

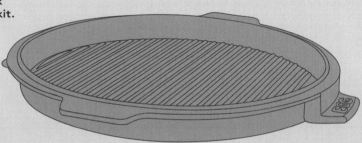

CONVEGGTOR®

A must-have for all BGE owners, this clever ceramic insert turns your EGG into a convection oven, for baking, slow-cooking, smoking, and roasting. The three-legged design stimulates heat circulation around the EGG without exposing food to the direct heat of the fire burning below.

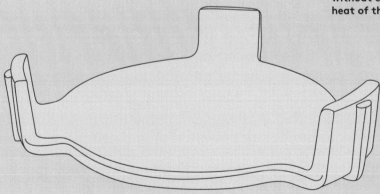

ALL IN PURSUIT OF FLAVOUR

Cooking with fire has been around longer than we've had language to write about it, but why does it still appeal? Why, when we've evolved kitchens, gas rings, microwaves and induction hobs, do we still drag out the 'barbecue' every summer and scorch proteins like Neanderthals?

For some, it's the atavistic appeal of flame and meat. The thrill of controlling fire seemingly never gets old and there can be few things so deeply satisfying as a sunny afternoon building up a good layer of char on a great cut of pork, but there's something else... something much more exciting going on. As we become more fascinated by diverse global food ways, and as the technology of fire cooking develops, we are suddenly more able to pursue subtleties of flavour. Today, cooking outdoors with fire doesn't have to be about blackening the outside of a steak or incinerating some cheap sausages. It's everything from the authentic 'bark' on a BBQ hog butt through a Korean bo ssam, from the delicacy of a Japanese yakitori to a Galician, slow-grilled turbot.

Outdoor fire cooking has become a key part of the repertoire of a new generation of chefs and food enthusiasts. Perhaps it still offers the macho flash of knife and flame, but now it's a new tool of subtlety, craft and – above all – flavour.

Physicists, firefighters, pyromaniacs and grill chefs will talk with great authority about the 'Fire Triangle', the three elements necessary for fire to ignite. They are heat, fuel and oxygen. Creating and controlling a fire means manipulating them all.

We'll talk in much greater depth later about how the Fire Triangle can be tamed, but first, let's consider another trio of factors – those controlling how the food will eventually taste – what you might call the 'Flavour Triangle'. The three elements that, in perfect balance, produce exactly the flavours you're seeking. These are the Fuel, Tools and Ingredients. The quality of ingredient you choose and how you prepare it, the fuel over which you cook it and the gear you use throughout the process all play a crucial role in this flavour triangle...

Let's look at these one at a time.

FUEL

Wood is the earliest form of fuel for cooking fires. There's a noble history of using dried animal dung too... but perhaps that avenue of culinary history is better left unexplored. Wood could be gathered from the ground or torn from plants but, in that state, it's not ideal for consistent cooking. Fresh-cut timber and anything that's lain around in the elements for a while will contain a fair amount of moisture either in the form of aromatic sap or just water, soaked into the fibres of the wood.

Damp wood is an incredibly inefficient form of fuel. It's heavy to carry and once the fire is burning, a large amount of energy is taken up in turning the moisture to steam. That hissing and spitting you hear when you toss a new log on the fire is water boiling, and the heat energy required for this boiling will not have been transmitted to the food. Some of the liquid in wood is more useful: oils, resins and other volatile compounds also burn off at low temperatures. Like any burning oil, they produce a thick, smutty smoke which sticks to things and hangs around as a delicious smell – as anyone who's spent an evening sitting round a campfire will know. Those fragrances and flavours will adhere as easily to food as they will to your clothes or hair and can be used brilliantly in low-temperature smoking – think salmon or pulled pork. But the aromatics are difficult to control. Allowed to burn too hard, they produce acrid, unpleasant flavours... which is why so much campfire food just tastes 'burnt' rather than tantalizingly 'smoky'.

It's doubtful that our ancestors were quite as enthusiastic about the taste of fire cooking as we are. And who can blame them? For them, smoke flavours were not a choice – sure, it's nice to have a smoky chop every now and again, but if every meal is tainted by the smell of damp wood from your local pine forest, things get pretty monotonous. It is for this, among other reasons, that cooks the world over grew to favour charcoal.

Charcoal is amazing stuff. It's light, easy to store, burns with total efficiency and produces little ash or smoke. It's so good at producing heat that it was used to smelt and forge metal.

Charcoal is made by clever manipulation of the Fire Triangle, by heating wood, in the absence of oxygen so it doesn't so much 'burn' as 'cook'. If wood is heated in an enclosed vessel, called a 'retort' both in the lab and in industrial production, then all of that inconvenient moisture and all the volatile elements of the wood are driven off. But because there's no oxygen, the wood doesn't actually combust but 'chars' into charcoal, a process called pyrolysis.

Traditionally, charcoal making has been done close to where the wood is harvested – there's no point shipping out heavy wet wood to process elsewhere when you can do the work close by and then just carry out the lighter charcoal. Across most of Europe, charcoal burners would cut wood and stack it into mounds before sealing it into a 'clamp' with damp soil to exclude air. A small fire would be set at the bottom of the pile and then the mound sealed, so the heat could spread through the pile, cooking and charring the wood. The charcoal burners could sit for up to a week watching the clamp, maintaining the outer surface, waiting and hoping that the process hadn't simply stopped or, worse, that air had entered, and the entire pile burned to ash.

Done right, the charcoal burners could turn several tons of cheap, damp wood into a smaller quantity of highly valuable pure fuel. But the slightest error and the entire investment could quite literally 'go up in smoke'.

Though there are still artisanal charcoal burners working in coppices, it is much more common for cooking charcoal to be produced by more modern and less risky methods. The cheapest charcoal 'briquettes' are made from carbon dust held together with a starch binder and sometimes even impregnated with accelerants to make them easier to light. If you want to scorch a sausage over a foil tray in a park, and you don't mind it tasting of kerosene, that's probably fine. Discerning home cooks, though, usually prefer 'lumpwood' charcoal. This is made from big chunks of hardwood, charred in retorts, sometimes using heat created by burning the volatile compounds from the wood itself. (Remember that turpentine, resin and tar can be extracted from wood so there's plenty of flammable stuff coming off to be used as fuel.) Lumpwood charcoal is beautiful to look at: black, shiny and with the original structure of the timber intact, almost like a fossil.

Restaurants and commercial BBQs need absolute consistency and cost-effectiveness in their charcoal. If you get up close to the grill, you'll see their charcoal is in the form of a hexagonal log with a hole through the centre, each piece the same size and density, with the maximum expanse of burning surface. These blocks are made by compressing sawdust under huge pressure and then pyrolizing in enclosed retorts. This technology was first developed in Japan in the 1960s and marketed as ogotan or ogalite, though it's now been adopted all over the world. It lacks some of the romance of artisanal charcoals, but it delivers the goods – perfect, consistent, repeatable heat.

The most premium and arcane of charcoals is the legendary Japanese binchō-tan, traditionally made in Wakayama Prefecture. It's made by heating ubame oak

in kilns at extremely high temperatures. It is so pure that if you knock two pieces together they will ring like bells. Binchō-tan burns with a high heat, without smoke, flame or smell. For small-scale, very precise benchtop grilling – the kind of thing you might do with tiny pieces of skewered protein over a konrō grill – binchō-tan is perfect, if very expensive. For Western grilling it would be largely wasted.

If you are of a scientific turn of mind, and you are still following, you might have noticed a slight flaw in our charcoal story. The cheapest and most basic charcoal has all the elements – that might give flavour – cooked out of it before use. More expensive charcoals are just purer.

However, more expensive charcoals are also an amazing source of clean heat. Depending on the wood used, well-made charcoals release slight variations in aroma that will compliment your food. There is also a certain amount of flavour generated when food drips onto the hot charcoal and creates smoke. BGE uses a blend of hickory and oak for their original lumpwood charcoal, but also produce a Canadian maple and Eucalyptus lumpwood – try each and see if you can notice subtle differences in the flavour of your food.

Just as better-quality lumpwood charcoals should be, the range manufactured by BGE does not have any added petroleums or chemicals to induce the burn process, ensuring you won't end up tasting the unpleasant taint that comes with cheaply manufactured charcoals. Investing in premium lumpwood means focusing on flavour and avoiding contaminating your food with unwanted chemicals and, in the case of BGE charcoal, ensures knowing that the wood used in production is organic and sustainably sourced.

If you want to increase the aromatic smokes of exotic woods beyond the reaches of charcoal, you have to add them back into the equation some other way. For most cooks, the most efficient and convenient way to do this is through the addition of wood chips.

Yes, I know, after all that effort to drive out moisture and volatile compounds from the wood, it might seem strange, but throwing a handful of well-soaked chips of applewood onto the hot charcoal will produce a small, controllable burst of smoke and steam, just enough to stick to the outside of the food as it cooks.

Apple, hickory, pecan, mesquite and cherry, are all easily obtainable, alder and cedar can add particular flavours to fish, while birch adds a kind of Scandinavian influence to food. And it's not just the chips that can be used. If you can find them, hay, fresh branches of juniper, rosemary or hyssop create bursts of flavours that might be challenging if overdone, but can be used subtly, to 'fine tune' flavour and significantly enhance good-quality charcoal, even transforming your BGE from grill to smoker. The possibilities are endless.

THE FIRE TRIANGLE

FUEL

FIRE

OXYGEN

HEAT

THE FLAVOUR TRIANGLE

INGREDIENTS

FLAVOUR

FUEL

TOOLS

TOOLS AND EQUIPMENT

1. MANAGING THE FIRE

It is possible to cook with fire and no tools at all. Many restaurants today will offer a 'dirty' steak on the menu, a piece of high-quality meat that's simply been seasoned and dropped onto the white-hot coals. This seems a little counter-intuitive, but the steak will, in fact, be anything but 'dirty', cooking at searing temperatures at which no pathogen could possibly survive. This is the origin point – the story of fire cooking stems from this very beginning.

Perhaps the next easiest way of cooking over fire, after dropping meat onto the coals, is to hold it over the flame so the rising heat can do its work without contact with ashes. The simplest method, as used by anyone who's ever sat round a campfire, is to support the food on a non-flammable skewer. This can be as simple as a green stick sharpened to a point and perhaps stripped of its bark. This enables the cook to bring the food in and out of the flame, up and down over the heat source. It's very controllable but requires constant attention and movement. You might be able to cook a few mouthfuls for yourself this way, but it's not a great way to manage dinner for the tribe.

To cook something larger, a whole beast or fish, it makes sense to craft a bigger skewer, push it through the carcass and arrange it in some way that it can be supported and rotated to avoid burning. An alternative is the very first ancestor of the modern grill, a platform woven of thin green sticks, used by Mesoamerican cultures, that could be used to cook lots of small things at once. It would only work over low heat as it was obviously combustible itself – the effect was probably more of smoking or drying than real grilling – but the basic principle was there. Some Spanish colonizers reported this technique as 'barbacoa', which is sometimes suggested as the root of the word 'barbecue'.

(Confusingly, Spanish colonists also used the term for another kind of long, slow pit cooking practised by the Taíno people of the Arawak-speaking Caribbean. This is also claimed as the root of American-style barbecue – low-temperature smoking and roasting.)

The equipment for all of these cooking methods could be created from wood and stone, and can predate the arrival of metal for utensils, which is why the development of the techniques is spread all over the world with all sorts of fascinating variations. It is incredibly difficult to track any fire-cooking method authoritatively back to a single point in culture or history.

With the arrival of metal, new types of cooking equipment were evolved. Grids and griddles could be fireproof, so food of all sizes could be cooked down over the flame and even possibly left unattended for a while. Metal plates could be used to sear meat without coming into contact with the flame, so carbonization (blackening) could finally be avoided. Spits and skewers now transmitted heat to the centre of the meat or fish, speeding up the cooking process and making it more even.

There can't be anyone in history who's cooked over a fire and not realized at some point that flame and heat cook differently. It's great to get a good layer of burn on the outside of a marshmallow or a piece of toast, but embers are where the action is. Where the flames have subsided, but the fiercest heat still remains, is the sweet spot where subtle work can be done. Over generations, cooks devised new and better ways to control this, to separate heat and flame, to create what outdoor cooks today would call 'indirect heat'. It is storing the heat in stones or bricks, long after the fire has died out, that gives us bread and pizza ovens. Keeping the fire outside and underneath a metal box is the basic principle that evolved into the domestic oven, which quickly dispensed with wood, coal or charcoal, as soon as clean and convenient gas and electricity came to domestic homes. Others devised deflectors – metal sheets that could 'bounce' heat from where the flame was burning to where the food would cook. Some used principles of convection, letting hot air move upwards from the heat source, around a baffle, and creating a fire-free area of clean, searingly hot air.

Every 'barbecue' we spark up in a garden or restaurant today is a part of one of these traditions – some descend from more than one. The simplest are trays and boxes that let us burn and control a fire. These can be disposable things made of aluminium foil, or more complicated benchtop set-ups with adjustable grill heights. It is easy to think of these simple models as cheap and amateurish but, in truth, this also describes a Greek souvlaki grill, an Argentine parilla, a Japanese konrō – all sophisticated tools that create some of the most exciting food in the world.

Today, many domestic users favour a barbecue with a lid. This amplifies the versatility. Of course, the heat can be contained, allowing for 'roasting', but perhaps more importantly, a lid shuts out airflow. When the fire is not 'open', the cook can use vents to admit more air above and below the coal bed, and effectively control the rate and temperature of burning. If the design of the unit is good and it's of a reasonable size, the cook can create hotter and colder 'zones' meaning more types of food can be cooked at once or, more usefully, so that 'indirect' heat can be achieved.

These are probably the most popular forms of outdoor grill in most of the West. They are a big piece of kit, reassuringly similar to a regular kitchen stove, they can be kept outdoors in all weathers, they're fairly easy to clean and they can even be powered by gas. They are commonly shaped like a coffin or a piano, depending on your turn of mind, or sometimes, near spherical – the 'kettle' barbecue popular across the USA.

They can be fitted with all sorts of attachments: planchas, rotisseries, wok rings and griddle racks, but nearly all these barbecues are made of metal, which is their main disadvantage. Sheet metal is an excellent conductor of heat and a very poor store of it. The outside of your barbecue will heat up very quickly and cool down just as fast. Sometimes, when cooking something that requires a quick burst of fast heat, this is perfectly acceptable but, for longer or more subtle cooking methods, it is a liability.

Consider how the average user cooks on the grill. We light it first, admit air, and the charcoal flares and then settles. We put on the food, which either cooks slowly or begins to get too brown too quickly. We adjust the position of the food, the vents, we add more fuel or scrape some away and the temperature changes... and keeps changing until we adjust it back again the other way. Every time you open the lid to check on the food, most of the contained heat shoots straight up into the clouds and it is only the charcoal itself that holds any heat over time. If you plotted a graph of heat against time in a regular metal barbecue, you'd see a wave pattern of rapid rises and falls – of limited amplitude if the cook is skilled, but all too often, chaotic. It's no wonder that the best way to cook on these grills is to catch one of those upward waves for fast, super-hot searing.

In other parts of the world, though, barbecues are made of other materials. A fire vessel made of ceramic has a much better ability to store heat than a metal one. Less fuel is used. The walls of the oven take longer to absorb heat but much, much longer to lose it. Changing the airflow does alter the temperature of the fire but the heat stored in the walls tends to even out variations. The graph is smoother and the heat more controllable. It was this type of grill, common over most of Asia, that inspired the Big Green Egg.

The Japanese word 'Kamado' is sometimes used to describe them, though in Japan, that refers to a domestic charcoal or wood cooking range, usually built from bricks. The kettle-shaped ceramic 'pot' oven was introduced to southern Japan from Korea and, over the last couple of decades, has become a serious contender for the ideal outdoor cooker.

As we learned in the Introduction, American serviceman and entrepreneur Ed Fisher was one of those who noticed the domed clay cooker and, impressed at how good the food tasted, began to import them to the US.

When Ed opened the first Big Green Egg store in Atlanta in 1974, the simple clay cooker he sold was based on the same design and materials that had been used thousands of years earlier.

Despite producing brilliant flavours, these original cookers were fragile and not durable enough to survive life in the garden so, as the EGG gained popularity, the company adapted the design to the new forms of heat-resistant ceramics that were then being developed by NASA for heat shields on space vehicles. The new EGG took man's oldest and most primitive form of cooking and applied 'rocket science' – resulting in a cooker that was stronger, more durable, and provided better heat insulation than anything else on the market.

BGE's programme of innovation didn't stop with the high-tech 'pot'. Every other element of the cooker was subject to an aggressive programme of research and innovation, increasing control and versatility. This means that the modern EGG is uniquely capable of replicating almost every kind of fire cooking imaginable, from dirty, 'down in the coals' caveman steaks to delicate Asian-inspired skewers of fish. It can cook huge complicated joints or challenging briskets, low and slow, then in minutes it can be reconfigured to cook pizzas on stones in a way that would pass muster with the master pizzaioli of Naples.

2. MANAGING THE COOKING

With the EGG putting you in total control of heat, it's time to turn our attention to the 'batterie de cuisine', equipment for cooking. This varies from thermometers to keep track of temperatures and the surfaces and gadgets you can cook the food on, to the tools for handling the food itself and various sundry bits and bobs that it's just handy to have around when you're cooking.

THERMOMETERS

There are many who quite justifiably shy away from technological gadgets in cooking, cleaving to tradition and loving the seat-of-the-pants skills required. This is fine, as long as we understand that cooking is about time and temperature and, if you're going to be a thermometer denier, you might as well ditch your watch too.

The EGG is equipped with a robust mechanical thermometer, drilled through the domed lid, which takes the temperature of the air inside the cooking space without your needing to open the lid. It's a simple piece of kit, based on a metal spring that coils or uncoils, according to how hot it gets, and drives a needle round a dial. The technology has been around since the Victorian era and is robust enough to work in industrial furnaces and forges. It's appropriate to the job but technology has given us more.

Chefs today rely not just on understanding the rough temperature of the oven but also the 'core temperature' of the food.

Let's take a common 'Sunday joint' as an example; say, a rolled beef topside – a useful example because of its regular texture and simple cylindrical shape.

Beef is cooked to medium-rare at 56.6°C/133.8°F. Our parents and grandparents would have placed a joint, perhaps a 20cm/8in diameter cylinder of solid meat, into a roughly 180°C/355°F oven and used guesswork, a recipe or experience to know how 'cooked' the centre was after a certain amount of time. It was a pretty rough estimation. If the joint was larger, it was perfectly possible for the outside to burn before the inside cooked (a common problem with poultry), which explains why so many recipes recommended draping foil over the meat during cooking.

This would also leave our theoretical joint with a 'temperature gradient'. When the centre hits 56.6°C/133.8°F, the surface is 180°C/355°F and everything else is in between. For many years cooks have believed in the awesome power of 'resting' meat – allowing the temperature gradient to even out as the centre cooks on and the surface cools – but by this point any attempt to predict the results becomes hopeless.

Modern chefs, tutored in the ways of 'molecular gastronomy', know that there is another way to heat the centre of the meat, perfectly to 56.6°C/133.8°F, and that is to put it in a cooking vessel at precisely 56.6°C/133.8°F and leave it there for ages. Not such a crazy idea when you think about it. The middle of the meat will 'eventually' get to temperature, it absolutely can't over-cook and you can always sear the outside later for an appealing crust.

The favoured way to do this is to seal the meat in a plastic bag and submerge it in a water bath. There are plenty of time charts available online to tell the chef the minimum cooking time for weight, but there's no maximum. The meat that comes out of the bag will be absolutely perfectly at the sweet point and only require a quick going over with a blowtorch, or, as many great chefs do, throwing it on a searingly hot BGE for a few seconds each side.

This kind of cooking, 'sous vide', has the terrific advantage that you need never eat a badly cooked steak in a restaurant ever again – there is no excuse for not getting the cuisson perfect – but it has also gifted us all with a greater understanding of the importance of core temperature.

Today a probe thermometer will set you back about £10–15 ($15–20), online or from a catering supplier. There is no longer any reason not to know the precise core temperature of what you're cooking, and so we can hope for an end to inaccurate recipes, overcooking

and BBQ food poisoning from undercooked chicken over the summer.

Of course, once you discover the thrill of being able to establish core temperature, there is a plethora of exciting technologies. Some manufacturers have fitted the probe to the end of an armoured, heatproof cable so the probe can stay jabbed into the food, the lid closed over it and the thermometer attached and hung outside the cooker. More advanced models use Bluetooth technology, so you can be chattering away, drink in hand, when your phone will alert you to the perfection of your pork butt.

The latest development at the time of writing is solid-state metal skewers containing their own transmitters, which let you keep an eye on several different dishes, or even different points on the same joint, to better create a temperature picture of the closed cooker.

The classic, old-style, mechanical thermometer in the lid of the Big Green Egg is superbly fit-for-purpose. It has the vintage rugged reliability of a classic camera or analogue watch. You can't quite yet sit on a deckchair, with a screen like Mission Control on your tablet, and be able to see your joint cooking and know the temperature of every single point at will... but it's surely only a matter of time.

HAND TOOLS

It feels like there are as many designs of barbecue hand tools as there are cooks to buy them. Many are expensive, but they don't need to be. The most important thing to remember is that you don't need anything to be frivolous.

Most cooks start with tongs. The problem here is that, of their nature, grill-cooking tools need to be long, to keep your hands out of the flame – and with long arms, the majority of BBQ tongs just can't take the torque. The food twists, the arms bend and the whole lot collapses.

Chefs favour cheap 'alligator' tongs: pressed stainless steel with jaws that spread into a kind of scalloped 'spoon' shape. They cost very little from your local catering supplier and can even come with silicon covers on the jaws. These seem to be resistant even to the heat of the EGG; they are amazingly robust and if they do eventually get a little loose and floppy, they're cheap to recycle and replace.

Alligator tongs, though, aren't hugely long. They are good for handling food a little off the fiercest heats but it's more sensible to modify the way you cook a little. You shouldn't need to reach down into a searing hot cooking chamber with tongs when the safer implements are the fork and hook.

A long, strong two-pronged BBQ fork is the key tool for shifting food about on a grill. As long as it's robustly made, it needn't cost much at all but it will be with you for ever. This can easily be long enough to reach right into the EGG while keeping your hands safely outside. And to really add to your dexterity, you need to look for the tool favoured by pitmasters and tandoori chefs: a long, sharpened hook. This can work as your 'other hand' and once you get used to it, allows remarkably fine operations.

Big Green Egg also has an excellent ash tool that looks like a Vegas croupier's 'rake', designed for cleaning out the ashes. You'll find yourself reaching for this surprisingly often when cooking, to back up your fork. A hook just increases the utility.

Finally, get yourself some gloves. Throw away anything with an amusing slogan on it – when was the last time you saw a welder wearing mittens marked 'Keep Calm and BBQ On'?

At various points, while cooking, you're going to have to move parts of the rig that will be much, much hotter than anything in a domestic cooking rig. Fortunately, technology has moved beyond the crazy 'mitten' design and there are now all sorts of hi-tech silicon gloves available. Most importantly, they allow you to use your fingers separately so you're not hampered by gigantic cartoon paws at precisely the moment you're juggling a red-hot cast-iron grill.

If you're a fan of technology there are excellent gloves knitted from 'Nomex' that are used by fighter pilots, firefighters and racing drivers. These are terrifyingly effective as long as they remain completely dry (see note on page 38).

BGE themselves have combined the technologies of the knitted fireproof glove with the benefits of silicon pads and grips in their proprietary EGGmitt. A dashing addition to your grilling wardrobe.

Another option is welder's gauntlets, made of a thick, unfinished leather. These stop welders, foundrymen, blacksmiths and metalworkers from burning themselves and should, therefore, cover most of the bases for an afternoon of light grilling.

Finally, it's worth, like every chef, having the habit of wearing two cloths, separated from each other, one on your belt and one over your shoulder. One of these is your 'wet' cloth, which can be used to mop things up, the other must not, under any circumstances get wet. This is the cloth you can fold up and use to handle hot pans. In professional kitchens there is a convention where the dry cloth is worn so, in an emergency, you can grab someone else's and be sure it's dry. Why...?

NOTE:

No matter what method you're using to protect your hands from heat, it will be useless if it gets wet. If cloth or gloves become even slightly damp, replace them immediately. In contact with heat, that water will turn immediately to steam, which can penetrate most cloths and gloves and can transmit heat far more aggressively than dry air. The worst kitchen burns occur when using a damp cloth to handle hot pans. This can be much worse in an enclosing glove. Be sure your hands are completely dry before putting gloves on.

HOLDING THE FOOD

Most BBQs and outdoor cookers come with a simple grill. These are most commonly made of a good-grade stainless steel that is easy to clean and has an element of non-stickiness about it. BGEs also come equipped with chunkier grills of cast iron. These heat up quickly and are great for putting attractive grill marks on meat or fish. But this is just the entry level of appliances for holding food, and it is in this department that the EGG, and its selection of carefully designed accessories, enables you to attempt the most interesting cooking methods from all around the world.

The grill, or part of it, can be replaced with a cast-iron or stainless-steel plate. This is usually called a 'plancha', which is the Spanish term, but it might equally well be a diner cook's griddle, a Japanese 'teppanyaki' grill, a classically trained chef's 'flat-top', or any one of a million skillet-type pans. Again, there is a choice between cast iron and stainless steel, which very much depends on your own favoured cooking style.

If you need to 'contain' the food, and possibly some liquid, you can obviously use a regular skillet on the grill, which is made more versatile by the addition of a close-fitting lid to enable steaming. It's also a good idea to have a 'Dutch oven' – a deep cast-iron pot that's favoured in African, Asian, American, South Asian and Caribbean cookery, but also functions as the familiar 'casserole' or as a small enclosed oven for vegetables or bread. Cast iron is the best material for both of these. Preferably uncoated... the jury is still out on how well a bright enamel surface survives the treatment.

With the heat in the EGG so controllable, it's possible to contemplate much subtler, more delicate cooking, for which the grill or plancha might be too aggressive. Metal baskets make fish much easier to handle when they might get torn apart by fork and tongs or stick to the grill. There are baskets for big round or flat fish and even ones specially designed for half a dozen sardines. Yakitori chefs also commonly use a device made of two wire mesh squares, loosely hinged at one side, with handles on the other. If your knife work is up to it, these are for food that's been cut into thin slices so it can be flashed quickly over the heat, turned then painted with a glaze or seasonings, then flashed again.

This technique of heating the food (particularly fish), cooling it a little with flavourings, then heating it again while constantly turning, is the basis of the Galician method of cooking whole turbot, where the fish is repeatedly painted with oil, water and salt. In the Argentine method for grilling whole sheep over fire, the animal is constantly flipped and doused with brine, which again slows the cooking and adds flavour.

For many years barbecue cooking has been regarded as a coarse and brutal art: big hunks of meat or whole fish combined with a lot of heat. But, often through the routes of Southeast Asian and Japanese cooking, we've discovered that very small grills are the key to even more interesting flavours and textures. The 'street food' treats we seek out when travelling and exploring are often cooked, in markets, over very small, highly controlled grills, fuelled by charcoal and often using skewers to support a single serving. Shish, souvlaki, suya, seekh, shawarma, satay, shashlik... and that's just the S's.

Marinades and flavourings can penetrate smaller pieces of meat or fish more efficiently and they can then be cooked much more quickly. The surface area is increased for crisping up and the skewer itself becomes the serving mechanism and only eating utensil. All of this obviously makes terrific economic sense for a street vendor but is also an inspiration to the grill cook. Skewers and some apparatus to support them make for great flavours, as long as you have good control of heat and you're prepared to keep the skewers moving.

Constant rotation of food is an age-old cooking technique with a couple of huge advantages. If you can keep a piece of meat rotating near a fire, the heat will be more regularly distributed, and you'll be less likely to burn something. The vertical rotisserie you'll see in a kebab joint takes advantage of this fact. But when meat is rotated on a horizontal axis, something even better happens. First, the bottom of the meat is heated by the fire, melting the fats and causing the juices to run, and then that part of the meat moves slowly to the top. The fats and juices, assisted by gravity, pour back over and through the joint, basting the meat while the underside is heating up... and the whole process continuously repeats. Electrically driven rotisseries are a game-changing addition to your EGG, keeping food juicy, reducing the possibilities of over or undercooking and even allowing you to take your attention off cooking for a while as the gentle process continues. It almost feels like cheating.

Finally, we should mention a couple of tools that aren't really part of the original BBQ rig but are, nonetheless becoming vital. With enclosed, lidded cookers capable of reaching extremely high temperatures, it didn't take enthusiasts long to work out they could be used as pizza ovens. Some used the pizza stones sold for domestic ovens and some manufacturers began supplying stones specifically designed to fit their

barbecues. The BGE, with a domed ceramic lid is a near-perfect replication of a pizza or bread oven and their own ceramic baking stones are able to reach high enough temperatures to create super-thin, crisp pizza bases in a matter of seconds – the holy grail of pizza making.

Equally exciting is the possibility of using woks over charcoal. A wok is designed for a very particular style of cooking. The bottom must be very hot and the food constantly stirred and tossed. The idea is that each piece is constantly rolled down into the hot zone for a very short time, then moved on by the cook, the action being repeated over and over again. The hemispherical shape means that the food rolls down under gravity and the cook's job is to repeatedly shovel it back up the sides. It's wonderfully clever and intuitive but, as home cooks have discovered, it's impossible to get high enough heat from a regular stove to properly use a wok.

Placing the wok over, or even in contact with, the charcoal in a barbecue creates the same kind of heat you'd get from a commercial wok burner and finally puts proper stir-frying and the tantalizing flavours of 'wok hai' in reach of the home cook.

MOPPING AND MARINATING

There's a variety of tools and techniques for adding moisture and flavours to food before and during cooking. Chief among them is the use of marinades, which can be applied in a variety of ways. Certain liquids, the acids in vinegar, wine, buttermilk or yogurt can actually begin to break down the meat to give a tenderizing effect as well as boosting its flavours. It should be handled carefully with delicate meats or fish. Marinating tandoori chicken in yogurt for half an hour or so doesn't really allow time for it to affect the meat at a structural level, while marinating it overnight reduces it to a kind of cotton-wool-like mush. Perhaps the chickens we're lucky enough to have for barbecuing today are less muscular and hard-worked than the creatures who ran around our ancestors' yards.

Some competition BBQ teams use injection to get marinade flavours and moisture into the fibres of the meat, and there are plenty of terrifying-looking syringe-like appliances available for this. The most important method of adding flavour, however, particularly where the temperature is properly controlled, is what pitmasters call 'mopping'. Think of the marinade as a more controllable basting medium. If it's made to the consistency of paint it can be daubed onto the surface with a mop or brush, with the intention that it should keep the surface lubricated and moistened, drying slowly in the heat. Mops are available in traditional cotton materials or more modern silicone, but a clean paintbrush is probably the simplest and cheapest method.

An Argentine parrillero will use a 'salmuera' on grilling food. It's a supersaturated salt solution, highly concentrated by boiling (garlic, chilli and herbs can be boiled in it too, then strained out before use). This is sprayed or splashed onto hot meat, where the moisture immediately evaporates, allowing salt to crystallize on the surface.

MISE-EN-PLACE

Finally, every cook preparing for service must prepare a 'mise-en-place': the collection of seasonings, sauces, spices and secret ingredients for fine-tuning the food to perfection. This should be entirely unique to every cook, but some elements are constant. It's good to have something to carry everything in. Some people have a toolbox, others a simple tray. It's a good idea to have a couple of spray bottles, one for salmuera if you're using it and one with plain water, to quell any inconvenient flare-ups. Oils and vinegars are best decanted into squeezy bottles, so you don't have to be fiddling with lids when your hands are full. A pepper grinder is vital and, because it can be used one-handed, this is probably the only time that a battery-operated grinder is not a ridiculous luxury. You'll need salt, obviously, and if you have a favourite proprietary or personal barbecue sauce, you'll want a big squeezy bottle of that too.

Have a stack of metal trays ready – the aluminium ones from a catering store are best. You can use these to hold your prepped ingredients but also to lift off cooked food for resting.

Keep one tray to hold your hand tools, your probe thermometer, mops, brushes, your gloves, cloths, a knife... and it's handy to have a roll of peach paper or aluminium foil around too.

SERVING

Try to plan well in advance, how the food is going to come to the table and be served. There's nothing worse than a confused scramble around cooling food while everybody tries to work out how it's going to be transferred to their plates. Serving spoons, forks and a carving knife should be out on the table already. Next to the cooking station you should have the right-sized plates, bowls, boards and covered dishes to get your finest work to the table. You know what size and shape the food will be when you're prepping it in the kitchen so there's no real need to be hunting for the right-sized dish as it's coming off the grill.

INGREDIENTS

Obviously the most important side of the flavour triangle is the ingredients we choose to cook. We are extremely fortunate to have access to more and more high-quality artisanal suppliers, most of whom understand fire cookery and are prepared to make good recommendations. Aside from the various hints and tips we'll go through below, the single most important one is to form a good relationship with your supplier. They are usually food enthusiasts themselves and will have all sorts of suggestions for interesting cuts and pieces… not all of them by any means expensive. The BGE is uniquely excellent for controlled, low, slow cooking and for extremely high-heat searing, which makes the variety of cuts for consideration even wider. Getting friendly with your butcher or fishmonger and taking time to chat with them will take your grill cooking to the next level.

There is one particular technique common to all meat and fish, which is worth discussing right upfront: the practice of 'early salting' – sometimes referred to as dry brining.

Many cooks have been taught that a good steak should only be salted or seasoned once it is on the grill, because otherwise valuable juices will leak out. It is true that if you salt the meat and leave it on a plate, a small pool of clearish pink liquid will form, but we now know that this is in fact predominantly water, not meat juice. Salt does remove moisture from meat – it's why we salt pork to make bacon – but in doing so it actually concentrates the remaining flavours.

Steaks, chops, chickens and even fish should often be salted well in advance of cooking, even overnight. If you can manage to do this uncovered in the fridge, so much the better. The fridge, with its cold dry air and circulating fans, dries the surface of the food, which will ensure a much crisper finish when it finally hits the grill.

BEEF

For a variety of historical and socio-economic reasons, we have come to regard beef as the premium meat we can buy. Many other cultures favour pork, lamb or bird, particularly in places where the cow is a useful draft animal. But for us, the big, ostentatious rib roast or a particularly fine and juicy steak speaks of luxury and indulgence.

If you are buying your beef from a decent butcher whom you trust, you shouldn't need to worry too much about ending up with meat from an intensively reared animal, but there are plenty of other variables, and plenty of other questions you can fruitfully ask.

Good butchers, these days, often offer a variety of beef from around the world and the choice can be bewildering, so here are a few starting tips.

A great deal of the best flavour in meat comes from fat, so the quality and distribution of the fat in the meat will be an indicator of quality. Good beef is 'marbled', meaning it has flecks of smooth fat running through it that will render during cooking and contribute to juiciness. If your butcher stocks Japanese Wagyu beef, you'll see it's so full of distributed fat that it's hard to distinguish the fibres of beef in between.

There are two principle ways that cattle are commercially reared for meat: grass-fed or corn-fed. The cow's natural diet is grass but it takes a very long time for an animal to grow to full slaughter weight by the inefficient process of cud-chewing. Corn-fed cattle are taken off pasture early in life and fattened on a diet of grain or soy. The grass-fed beef you buy will likely come from older animals. The fat will be yellowish. The meat flavour will be complex – some people say more fragrant, others more acidic. The meat texture tends to be firmer, as you'd expect from an older beast who's ranged over fields.

Corn-finishing cattle is a highly industrialized process in the US and is not universally popular with cooks. However, some small artisanal farmers also corn-finish on a much more humane scale. Because the animal reaches slaughter weight faster, the meat is usually more tender, marbled through with a whiter fat and has a taste that most categorize as 'buttery'.

To add depth and complexity to the flavour of the meat, it can be hung, sometimes just for a few days, but it's not unusual for butchers to offer meat that's been hung for up to 90 days.

Hanging is expensive for butchers. Hang a 70kg (155lb) side for a few days, uncovered in a fridge, and it will begin to dry out… to literally lose weight. A premium piece that's been aged for weeks may end up being only 75% of its original weight, and that means that the price goes up.

As the meat dries, its flavours concentrate, but there's also a slow process of lacto-fermentation happening inside the meat that both tenderizes it and adds really complicated flavours that vary between umami and a kind of cheesy funk. Long-hung meat can be a little challenging, but a short period of ageing can improve almost any beef.

Some aficionados prefer a lot less ageing on corn-fed meat as it's already tender and its flavour is subtle.

Finally, discuss with your butcher the 'complexity' of the piece of meat you are buying. Generally speaking, cuts from higher up on the back of the beast and towards the rear are simpler. They tend to be large chunks containing just one or two well-worked muscles. Rump, sirloin, chateaubriand, fore-rib and silverside all feature the huge muscles that keep a couple of tons of cow standing up all day. They can usually be cooked more quickly, at higher temperatures, and would be the traditional centrepieces for a large meal.

But it's also important to look at the other end of the carcass, lower and towards the front. Pieces like brisket, clod, flank and ribs are much more complicated collections of smaller muscles, some bone, fat and connective tissue. Real grill experts delight in these cuts because they are cheap, and, when they're cooked for a very long time at very low temperatures on the EGG, they reward with superb textures and much more interesting flavours than the premium pieces.

PORK

Some of the rules of choosing pork are similar to those for beef. Cuts on the beast's back and towards the rear have usually been regarded as the best in the past; in fact, the term 'to live high on the hog' means to treat oneself to the best pieces. Traditionally, farmers would use the butt and back legs to make high-quality hams that could be sold for good money, while the family would salt down the forelegs, shoulders and belly as salt-pork or bacon, for their own consumption.

Pigs lay down fat throughout their bodies but build up spectacular layers just below the skin. This is obviously great for grill cooking as the tough skin tends to crackle up and protect the meat from burning while the fat renders and self-bastes the meat to keep it moist.

A word of warning. Beef steaks and chops are easy to grill and can be quite forgiving, but small pieces of the premium cuts of pork are incredibly easy to dry out and dry pork is nobody's idea of fun. The easiest ways to avoid drying out are to make sure you don't trim the fat before cooking (do it just before serving if you must) and remove from your mind the fear of undercooking pork. Sustainably reared pork is not as riddled with bad things as the factory-produced stuff, so it doesn't need to be incinerated for safety.

The British Food Standards Agency currently advise a core temperature of 75°C/167°F for pork, but they don't distinguish between the quality of pork involved. The current American standard is 63°C/145°F and a few minutes of rest before serving, which will certainly ensure a juicy chop.

Once again, cuts from low down and towards the animal's head can yield terrific results with low and slow cooking. The pork belly is a laminated slab of muscle sheets, fat, connective tissue and soft gelatinous bones that can be cooked to the most unctuous softness. It takes a long time to bring all those constituent elements to the perfect texture for eating, but it's truly worth the wait.

Perhaps the favourite pork joint for outdoor cooking, though, is the shoulder. The blade bone, passing through the middle of the meat, about the size of a shovel, conveys gentle heat right to the middle of the joint where it slowly renders all the complicated parts around the main joint. A really well-cooked shoulder comes to the table with a crisped outer shell of crackling that barely contains the falling-apart juiciness inside. Don't carve it, just show it a fork.

If your butcher can get it, 'Iberico' pork is particularly good. For centuries, farmers in Extremadura in Spain have let their blackfoot pigs feed on foraged acorns in the dry scrub of the area. Their legs are used to make the prized air-dried hams of the region but only recently have the farmers begun exporting the cuts they don't use for 'jamón'. The cuts are different from what many of us are used to, with names like 'secreto' and 'presa', and the meat is so dark and intensely flavoured from the acorn diet, that many people often mistake grilled Iberico pork for very good-quality beef.

LAMB

For many years there was almost no tradition of lamb cookery in the US at all. In the UK it's long been eaten, probably a by-product of the national wool industry, but it is also, to be fair, the most polarizing of the meats. Sheep range in the open for most of their lives and largely eat pasture that doesn't require massive chemical intervention. Not all lamb is free-range but most of it is pretty close. But it's also a particularly fatty meat, with a pronounced sweetness of flavour. It's easy to see how some find it too rich.

A smaller beast than a cow or pig, a sheep can't really offer a large number of substantial premium back cuts. Lamb chops or rack are the obvious choice, or the fillet – effectively the same muscle cut in a different direction. These can actually be cooked rare. The leg provides a good-looking celebratory joint, impressive to carve at the table, or for easier flavouring and faster cooking, the leg can be 'butterflied' – trimmed out into a large flat piece of reasonably even thickness. The shoulder, like the pork shoulder, is best cooked slowly so it can be pulled apart to serve.

Lamb and goat are the principal eating meats across the Muslim world. Recipes rarely treat lamb as we do (as a free-standing joint) because in stews, ragus, tajines, or cooked on skewers, smaller pieces of lamb can be better spiced to cut the fatty richness.

We have become used to eating young lambs here in the UK, which is a shame because their meat gains more character as they get older. A lamb is less than a year old at slaughter. An animal slaughtered between one and two years is called a hogget, and if your butcher ever offers you any, snap it up. It's rare to find mutton in a butcher's these days because the expense of rearing an animal for two or more years can't be reflected in the price, but it's completely delicious and grills beautifully.

CHICKEN

Chicken has always been a popular meat to grill but it's not the easiest to get right. Chicken breasts are a perfect serving size and easy to eat but can dry out very quickly if even slightly overcooked. Drumsticks, on the other hand, are wiry little bundles of muscle and sinew that really need slow cooking to properly melt,

Wings are fiddly but completely enjoyable to eat, kids particularly like smearing them all over the place, but the thigh meat is probably the best all-rounder for grilling. With the bone removed and opened out flat, the thigh is a single disc of very juicy, dark meat, with a good mixture of textures and a layer of skin on one side that crisps up perfectly. Put a couple of slim metal skewers through the thigh if you want to be absolutely sure of cooking through.

A great benefit of the BGE is how well it roasts, or partially smokes, whole chickens. The usual difficulty with roasting any bird is that the breast will be overdone and dry before legs and thighs have had enough time to cook through. The domed lid of the EGG creates a perfectly chicken-sized enclosure. With its huge thermal mass, and with the convEGGtor in place, it lets you cook the whole bird gently and slowly, with very regular and consistent heat on all sides.

FISH

There is nothing more glorious than the smell of fish on a hot grill. It's so delicate that it requires little time, but it particularly benefits from direct heat cooking. Unlike meat grilling, which can be a robust process, fish cookery is all about protecting. The skin protects it from the fiercest heat while the fish steams in its own plentiful juices inside.

Ideally, you'll need good thick chunks of fish, with skin still on, scales removed and bones in place. Neatly trimmed fillets will, frankly, collapse in seconds. Round fish like sea bream or salmon, are good cut straight across into thick slices, but, if the number of guests justify it, it's always better to go for whole fish. They don't just look great as you bring them to the table but the intact skin all round will protect the empty cavity, where the fish has been gutted, which can be packed with aromatics.

Flat fish, like halibut or turbot grill extremely well, though they do need special attention so they can be supported over the fire (see page 78).

If you have to cook small or delicate pieces of fish, you can wrap them, with aromatics, in pouches made of foil or peach paper, but, as that means keeping the food out of contact with the fire, it seems a shame.

Finally, don't neglect oily fish. Mackerel, sardines or pilchards have tougher skins and oilier flesh. Get the grilling temperature right and they effectively fry themselves in their own oiliness. Unfortunately, oily fish don't last brilliantly well once they've been caught so, they should certainly be a special treat if you can source them from fishermen or catch them yourself, but, once again, if you trust your fishmonger and ask the right questions, you may well be able to get mackerel or sardines that were properly frozen as they were caught.

Finally, don't neglect prawns (shrimp), mussels, oysters, scallops or lobsters. Shellfish and crustacea come in their own serving containers and can be placed straight onto the grill bars. All that extra salty moisture boils up and steams the flesh to perfection.

THE FIRST RECIPE:
Chicken Wings

SERVES 2–4
(4–8 wings per person)

EGG SET UP
Indirect set-up; convEGGtor in legs-up position with the stainless-steel grill on top of the convEGGtor legs.

TARGET TEMP
190–220°C / 375–430°F

This was Ed Fisher's first cook on the Big Green Egg, before they were properly Big Green Eggs. I've gone for a simple recipe here, just to ease you in, but chicken wings are versatile and can take just about any flavour. Try your favourite rub or experiment a little – I like Chinese-style with ginger, garlic, soy, chilli and honey. This recipe works equally well with drumsticks; it's good to flatten the middle section with drumsticks, but you don't have to, and add a few minutes extra of cooking time.

1.5kg / 3lb 5oz chicken wings (about 12–15)

3 tbsp olive or vegetable oil

1 tsp salt

½ tsp freshly ground black pepper

1 tbsp ground cumin

1 tbsp ground coriander

1–2 tsp chilli powder

For the basting mix

3 garlic cloves, very finely chopped

30g / 1½ tbsp honey, or 2 tbsp brown sugar

Juice of 1 lemon or 2 limes

Pat the wings dry and rub with the oil, salt, pepper and spices. Mix the baste ingredients together.

Place the chicken on the grill in a single layer, close the lid and leave for 15 minutes, then baste, turn the wings over and cook for another 10–15 minutes, basting twice more.

Cook until ready, with an internal temperature of 74°C / 165°F, or when the skin feels like it's lifted away from the flesh and the flesh in the middle section pulls away from the bone.

ROAST CHICKEN TO BRISKET

12 recipes to take you from EGG beginner to BBQ rockstar.

This section of the book is based on the premise that we all want to be a BBQ rockstar. Of course we do, but mastering the EGG takes time, practice and patience. What follows are 12 recipes, a 12-step programme if you like, to take you from novice to pro. Aaron Franklin of the world-famous Texas restaurant Franklins BBQ once said: 'You only learn how to make good BBQ by making bad BBQ.' If you start at roast chicken and take each recipe in turn you will learn all the skills and gain the confidence you need to be that rockstar, and minimize the amount of bad BBQ along the way.

COOK NO. 1

BEGINNER

SERVES 4–6

EGG SET UP
Indirect set-up; convEGGtor in legs-up position with the stainless-steel grill on top of the convEGGtor legs.

TARGET TEMP
170–200°C / 340–390°F

ROAST CHICKEN

Roasting a chicken is something most of you will be familiar with. There is a succulence and juiciness the EGG gives a roasted chicken that means you will never return to a conventional oven. Here you are setting up the EGG at its most basic, as a roasting oven, at a temperature that will serve you well for cooking lots of different ingredients.

I like to cook my chicken on a rack over a roasting pan with an inch or two of water in it. As the chicken cooks it will drip roasting juices into the water. This becomes a stock that can serve as the base of a gravy. The water also helps keep the atmosphere inside the dome moist, which in turn helps keep the chicken moist. It's a technique than can be applied to most meat-roasting recipes, but is by no means essential.

1 chicken, 1.5–2kg / 3lb 5oz–4lb 6oz, removed from fridge before lighting the EGG

2 garlic cloves, unpeeled and squashed slightly

½ lemon, halved into 2 quarters

1 big sprig of rosemary, thyme or sage

1 tbsp olive oil

Salt and freshly ground black pepper

Pat dry the chicken and generously season the cavity with salt and pepper, then pop in the garlic cloves, one piece of lemon and the herb sprig. Rub the chicken with the juice from the remaining lemon quarter and the olive oil, then generously season on all sides with salt and pepper.

Place the chicken either directly on the grill or in a roasting pan, breast side up. Close the lid and roast for 1–1½ hours until the skin is crisp and golden brown and the meat is cooked through – the internal temperature should read 74°C / 165°F.

Transfer the chicken to a large plate and let it rest for about 20 minutes before carving or jointing to serve.

STEAK

A few notes on cooking steak... It needs to be at room temperature before you start cooking it. Season the steak heavily, preferably with flaky sea salt. I once watched Richard Turner, of Hawksmoor and Meatopia fame, and a man who has forgotten more about cooking meat than I'll ever know, toss his huge Tomahawk steaks in sea salt before putting them on the grill. That is how well you need to season your steak. I know you will want to watch your steak being cooked, but you can't. In between turning, it is essential you keep the lid closed. As the fat on your steak melts, it will drip onto the charcoal below. If you leave the lid open, the fat will ignite, causing a flare-up. The flame direct on the steak's fat will cause it to burn and give an acrid coating of smoke to your meat. The way around this is to keep the lid shut, starving any potential flames of oxygen. When you need to turn the steak, burp the EGG (see page 12), then lift, turn and close. Ensure you preheat the grill or grid before you add the steak.

SERVES 2

EGG SET UP
Direct set-up with the stainless-steel grill (or cast-iron grid if you have one) on top.

TARGET TEMP
220–260°C / 430–500°F

2 steaks, cut 4cm / 1½in thick, removed from fridge before lighting the EGG	Salt (flaky sea salt or fleur de sel is best)
	Coarsely ground black pepper

Pat the steaks dry just before cooking as they will be a bit damp.

Season the steak generously with salt and pepper, place on the grill, close the lid and cook for about 1½ minutes on each side until both sides are nicely browned. Then, for 650g/1lb 7oz rib-eye/sirloin (short-loin), cook for 6–8 minutes more for rare, 8–10 minutes for medium, and 10–12 minutes for well done (or see the internal temperature chart below), burping the EGG and turning halfway through the cooking time.

Allow the steak to rest somewhere warm for 10 minutes before slicing to serve.

TEMPERATURE TEST FOR DONENESS
Cook the steak to the following internal temperatures before resting:

Rare: 50–55°C / 122–131°F
Medium-rare: 55–58°C / 131–136°F
Medium: 58–63°C / 136–145°F
Medium-well done: 63–68°C / 145–154°F
Well done: 68°C / 154°F+

COOK NO.3

BEGINNER

SERVES 4

EGG SET UP
Make the dough before lighting the EGG.

Indirect set-up; convEGGtor in legs-down position with the baking stone in place.

TARGET TEMP
275–325°C / 530–620°F

PIZZA

Cooking pizza takes some practice. The art is to get the base crispy but not quite burnt while cooking the toppings. Remember it is essential you allow the EGG long enough to heat the baking stone or you won't get the crispy base. I cannot stress enough how important it is that you wait until you get to the right temperature. If you don't, you will be scraping half-cooked dough from your baking stone, rather than enjoying delicious pizza. Mastering pizza will allow you to bake all manner of breads, something that will come in handy later in the book, as well as being able to manage the EGG at a high temperature. I am grateful to Luke Vandore-Mackay for polishing my EGG pizza skills.

500g / 4 cups '00' flour (or 400g / 3 cups '00' flour and 100g / ⅔ cup semolina flour), plus extra for dusting

1 tsp fast-action dried yeast

1 tsp salt

350ml / 1½ cups water

For the topping
500g / 1lb 2oz new potatoes, thinly sliced

2 sprigs of rosemary, needles roughly chopped

2 tbsp extra-virgin olive oil, plus extra to drizzle

3 garlic cloves, finely chopped

250g / 9oz mozzarella, cut or torn into little pieces

Freshly grated Parmesan

Salt and freshly ground black pepper

Make the dough. Put the flour, semolina flour if using, yeast and salt in a big mixing bowl and stir in the water with a spoon. Mix well to combine completely, place a damp cloth over the bowl and leave for an hour or so until almost doubled in size.

Mix the sliced potato with half the rosemary, the olive oil and some salt, and spread out in a thin layer in a baking tray. Bake in the hot EGG for 5 minutes until softened and beginning to brown at the edges. Toss with the garlic and the remaining rosemary and check for seasoning, then leave to one side.

Divide the dough into 4 even pieces and roll into balls. Place on a lightly floured tray. Have a pizza peel or thin board ready, and dust lightly with flour.

Roll or stretch one ball of dough into a round base about 30cm / 12in in diameter. Transfer it to the peel and top with a quarter each of the potato and mozzarella, and a sprinkling of Parmesan.

Slide the pizza onto the hot baking stone, close the lid and cook for 4–8 minutes (this really does depend on temperature; as you open and close the EGG the temperature can rise quite quickly).

Slide the cooked pizza onto a large plate or a chopping board and top with a little more olive oil and some salt and pepper, followed by some more freshly grated Parmesan. Repeat with the remaining pizza dough and topping. You can completely play around with toppings to suit your tastes – for a classic margherita, swap the potatoes for tomato passata.

COOK NO.4

BEGINNER

SERVES 6–8

EGG SET UP
Indirect set-up; convEGGtor in legs-up position with the stainless-steel grill on top of the convEGGtor legs. You'll need a Dutch oven.

TARGET TEMP
130–150°C / 265–300°F

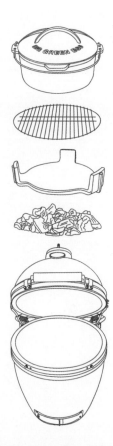

GOAT SHOULDER POMEGRANATE RAAN

Goat has a special place in my heart, as in my other life I own and run a goat meat business that takes unwanted male 'kid' goats and puts them into the food system via restaurants, catering butchers and an online shop. These animals were once routinely euthanized for lack of demand, which is a terrible and immoral waste. This recipe brings out the best in the goat and will get you comfortable with slow cooking to spoon-soft, 'pullable' meat.

This is as much a test of your patience as it is a test of your cooking skill. The maxim 'if you're looking, it's not cooking' applies here. Opening the lid to check your cook upsets the temperature of the EGG, which can have dire consequences, not necessarily with this recipe, but later when you are cooking with more sensitive ingredients.

1 bone-in shoulder of kid goat (or lamb), about 2.5kg / 5½lb

1 large onion, thinly sliced

Oil, for brushing

40g / 4¾ tbsp ghee or butter

100ml / generous ⅓ cup pomegranate juice (or use 2 tbsp pomegranate juice topped up with water)

30g / ⅓ cup flaked (slivered) toasted almonds, lightly crushed

Seeds of ½ pomegranate

Small bunch of coriander (cilantro), roughly chopped

For the marinade

100g / scant ½ cup plain full-fat yogurt

2 tbsp (or more to taste) tandoori spice blend (page 60)

4 garlic cloves, finely chopped

2 tbsp finely grated fresh ginger

Juice of 1 lemon

1 tsp salt

To serve

Quick pickled red onions (page 182)

Paratha (page 173)

Raita (page 187)

Zhug (page 190)

Combine the marinade ingredients in a bowl and mix together well. Place the goat shoulder in a Dutch oven or heavy oven pot and spread three-quarters of the marinade over all sides of the meat. Lift the joint and place the sliced onion underneath, resting the meat on top. Cover and place in the fridge overnight, or for a minimum of 2 hours, bringing it to room temperature before cooking.

Oil the grill lightly and place the goat directly on the grill (reserve the onion and marinade in the pot). Close the lid and cook for around 1½–2 hours until the marinade has set and formed a crust.

Continued overleaf

Remove the goat from the grill and place the onions in their pot on the grill, adding the ghee or butter. Cook for 10–15 minutes until golden, then remove from the grill and add the meat back to the pot. Brush with the reserved marinade and add the pomegranate juice to the pot. Sprinkle over half the almonds, check the seasoning, cover in a double layer of foil and return to the EGG for 1½–2½ hours until the meat is meltingly tender, and the bone easily slides away from the meat.

Remove from the EGG and rest for 30 minutes, then sprinkle with the pomegranate seeds, chopped coriander and remaining almonds to serve. You can either shred the goat, or serve it whole, with your choice of accompaniments.

TANDOORI BLEND (MAKES ABOUT 4 TBSP)

2 tsp ground coriander
2 tsp ground cumin
2 tsp ground turmeric
1–3 tsp Kashmiri chilli powder (or another chilli powder), depending on the heat you prefer
1 tsp smoked paprika
½ tsp amchur (mango) powder
½ tsp freshly ground black pepper
1 tsp salt
¼ tsp dried mint
¼ tsp dried fenugreek leaves
¼ tsp ajwain or black cumin seeds (optional)

SMOKED MACKEREL

This recipe has you smoking, managing low temperatures to make the smoke flavour the showcase of the dish. This can be scaled up to suit any oily fish; smoking sides of salmon or trout and presenting them on the wooden grilling plank they were smoked on is a showstopper of a summer dish (find these on the Big Green Egg website). The addition of wood chips would add extra smoke flavour to the fish, and there is great debate as to whether to pre-soak your wood chips in water or not. It makes little difference, but if you do, give them 30 minutes' soaking time. If you are plank cooking, pre-soak the plank for 30 minutes.

SERVES 4

EGG SET UP
Salt the mackerel before lighting the EGG.

Indirect set-up; convEGGtor in legs-up position with the stainless-steel grill on top of the convEGGtor legs.

TARGET TEMP
100–120°C / 210–250°F

4 medium-sized fresh mackerel, either filleted or butterflied (opened like a book)

30g / 1oz coarse sea salt

30g / 2 tbsp light brown sugar

1 tsp fennel seeds, crushed

1 tsp cracked black pepper, plus extra pepper to serve

Grated zest of 1 lemon, plus a few drops of juice to finish

1 bay leaf, thinly sliced

2 tbsp sherry (optional)

Oil, for brushing

Lay out the fish skin-side down in a non-reactive tray and carefully remove the pin bones.

Scatter the dry ingredients and flavourings evenly over the fish, and sprinkle over three-quarters of the sherry, if using. Cover and leave for 15–30 minutes, then rinse and pat dry.

Brush the grill with oil and add the mackerel. Close the lid and cook for 12–15 minutes until just cooked through. It should be opaque, and a metal skewer should easily go through the fish. If it requires more cooking, transfer back to the grill on a tray for a few minutes.

Carefully lift the fish onto a plate and coarsely grind over some black pepper, then sprinkle over the remaining sherry, if using, and a few drops of lemon juice.

Serve straight away or at room temperature with new potato salad, or squashed onto toast.

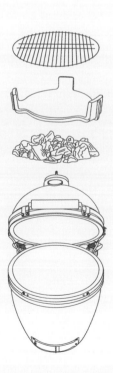

COOK NO.6

SERVES 4

EGG SET UP
Direct set-up with the
stainless-steel grill in place.

TARGET TEMP
170–210°C / 340–410°F

BRINED CHICKEN BREAST

Brining is a useful skill; soaking in a salt solution locks moisture into meat and is especially useful for poultry, which has a tendency to dry out if it's not cooked precisely. Once you are comfortable with brining and you taste the difference it makes, you'll want to experiment. And you'll want to do it again and again.

This recipe also has you direct cooking as you did with the steak a few steps back. The difference is the chicken isn't as robust and will need a low temperature and more time; controlling the direct heat will keep you from burning it (but be sure to preheat the grill properly). You can also brine chicken thighs this way, but cook them until the internal temperature reads 74°C / 165°F.

4 large boneless, skin-on chicken breasts

For the brine
30g / 1oz coarse salt
150ml / ⅝ cup boiling water
2 tbsp spices (I use a mixture of black pepper, fennel seeds, chilli, paprika and dried oregano)

3 garlic cloves, crushed
Finely grated zest of 1 lemon
2 tbsp chopped herb leaves (I use a mixture of bay, thyme and rosemary)
150ml / ⅝ cup cold water

In a bowl, mix the salt with the boiling water, spices, garlic, lemon zest and herbs, until the salt is dissolved, then add the cold water and allow to cool.

Add the chicken and allow to brine for 20–30 minutes in the fridge, then remove the chicken from the brine, pat dry and bring back to room temperature.

Add the chicken to the grill, close the lid and cook for 10–12 minutes per side, until the internal temperature reads 71°C / 160°F. Cut into slices to serve.

COOK NO. 7

INTERMEDIATE

SERVES 6–8

EGG SET UP
Indirect set-up; convEGGtor in legs-up position with the stainless-steel grill on top of the convEGGtor legs.

TARGET TEMP
130–150°C/265–300°F,
then 180–200°C/355–390°F

PORK BELLY
with Membrillo Alioli

Now we're getting into the swing of things. Pork and smoke are a wonderful combination and one of those classic BBQ flavours. I'm guessing that when you bought your EGG, a big hunk of pork was on your list of things to cook first. With this recipe you are managing a temperature change during the cook. You will find yourself having to do this to crisp up, sear or finish a dish in plenty of recipes. This works equally well with a boned and rolled pork collar roasting joint.

Adding wood chips here is very much a matter of personal taste. I think it can get a bit much on slow cooks, and if you are using a quality charcoal there is plenty of flavour already. I suggest you master these recipes without wood chips and then experiment once you are confident. That way you will have a base flavour to compare 'chips vs no chips', safe in the knowledge you have not made a mistake in the cooking process.

Piece of pork belly or collar, about 1.5kg/ 3lb 5oz, removed from fridge before lighting the EGG, skin scored with a sharp knife

For the membrillo alioli
1 plump garlic clove
250g/9oz membrillo (quince paste)

150ml/⅝ cup oil (equal parts extra-virgin olive oil and sunflower oil)
Lemon juice, to taste
Salt and freshly ground black pepper

Season the joint all over with salt and pepper on the flesh side. Place on the grill skin side up, close the lid and roast for 1½–2 hours, until the internal temperature of the meat reaches about 60–65°C/ 140–150°F.

While the pork is roasting, peel and crush the garlic with a little salt then add to a blender. Add the membrillo and blend slowly, adding the oil in a thin stream, stopping a few times, until all the oil is emulsified into the membrillo. Add salt, pepper and lemon juice to taste.

Increase the temperature of the EGG to 180°C/355°F and turn the pork skin side down to crackle the skin. Check every 2 or 3 minutes, moving it away from any hot spots near the edge if it looks like it might scorch before crackling.

Allow to rest for 20 minutes before carving or slicing and serving with the membrillo alioli.

DUTCH OVEN BONE-IN VEAL SHIN PASTA

Cooking in a pot inside a Big Green Egg is a joy. Many of the classic dishes you know from your conventional oven get an extra layer of complexity in the EGG, and this shin dish is one of them. In a conventional oven you would brown the meat in the same pot as you'd cook it in. If you wanted to do that here the EGG would need to get really hot. Too hot to then cook the meat. Instead you brown the meat on the grill, which gives it that punch of smoky flavour, while you are softening the vegetables in the pot. Once you've got the hang of this, all the stews and braises in your repertoire will be destined for the Big Green Egg Dutch oven method.

If you can't find veal, beef shin will substitute well. If using veal, this can be served unshredded as osso buco, topped with gremolata (page 189).

SERVES 6

EGG SET UP
Indirect set-up; convEGGtor in legs-up position with the stainless-steel grill on top of the convEGGtor legs. You'll need a Dutch oven.

TARGET TEMP
140–160°C / 285–320°F

4 tbsp olive oil

4 pieces of veal osso buco (or use diced beef shin), removed from fridge before lighting the EGG

1 onion, finely chopped

2 carrots, finely chopped

2 small leeks, finely chopped

1 head of garlic, cloves peeled and finely chopped

200ml / generous ¾ cup dry white wine

1 tbsp tomato purée (paste)

2 sprigs of sage, leaves finely chopped

500ml / 2 cups chicken stock

Small bunch of flat-leaf parsley, leaves finely chopped

400g / 14oz dried pappardelle pasta

70g / 2½oz Parmesan, finely grated

Salt and freshly ground black pepper

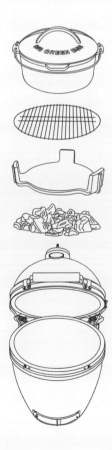

Preheat a Dutch oven or cast-iron pot in the EGG for 10 minutes, then add the oil to the pot and allow to preheat for 2 minutes.

Season the meat with salt and pepper and place straight on the grill. Cook for 10 minutes to lightly brown, turning once. At the same time, add all the chopped vegetables and garlic to the pot to soften for 15–20 minutes, stirring a few times.

Pour the wine into the pot with the tomato purée, sage and stock and bring to the boil, then place the browned meat in the pot. Close the lid of the EGG and cook for 3–4 hours, without the pot's lid, until the meat is very tender, but not falling apart, adding a splash of water or more stock if it dries out. Stir through the parsley and shred the veal using two forks, discarding the bones (or keep the meat whole if you prefer). Check the seasoning, adding salt and pepper to taste. Keep warm.

Cook the pasta until al dente, according to the packet instructions, then drain well, reserving a little cooking water. Add the hot pasta to the veal with a couple of tablespoons of pasta water and toss. Serve topped with the Parmesan.

COOK NO.9

EXPERT

SERVES 8–10

EGG SET UP
Indirect set-up; convEGGtor in legs-up position with the stainless-steel grill (or cast-iron grid if you have one) on top of the convEGGtor legs.

TARGET TEMP
93–135°C / 200–275°F
(ideally 120°C / 250°F),
then 240–270°C / 465–520°F

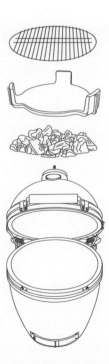

STANDING RIB ROAST

A classic Sunday lunch and one of the marquee cooks of which we all dream. It's a cook that takes planning and patience and a few of the skills you've learned in the 8 steps you have taken to get to here: managing the EGG at a low temperature, changing gear mid-cook by raising the temperature, and patience. It can take hours, but that's no bad thing.

I think rib is at its best when it's cooked medium-rare or medium (54°–58°C / 130–136°F) but cook rare if you prefer. This is another cook where standing the meat on a wire rack on a roasting pan with an inch or two of water in it will help retain moisture and give you a base for gravy.

1 bone-in fore-rib of beef, removed from fridge before lighting the EGG

Flaky sea salt

To serve
Crème fraîche
Horseradish

Season the beef all over with a very generous amount of salt. If you have the opportunity, leave it like this overnight in the fridge (and bring back to room temperature to cook), but if that's not possible then salt at least an hour before cooking.

Place the beef fat side up on the grill, close the lid and cook for 4–5 hours, until the internal temperature is 50°C / 120°F for rare, 54°C / 130°F for medium-rare or 58°C / 136°F for medium. Wrap in foil and leave somewhere not too cold for at least 30 minutes or up to 1 hour.

Carefully remove the convEGGtor, then increase the heat to 240–270°C / 465–520°F. Unwrap the beef and colour it in the EGG for 3–5 minutes, then leave to rest for 5 minutes. Sprinkle with more flaky salt, then serve with crème fraîche mixed with a little horseradish.

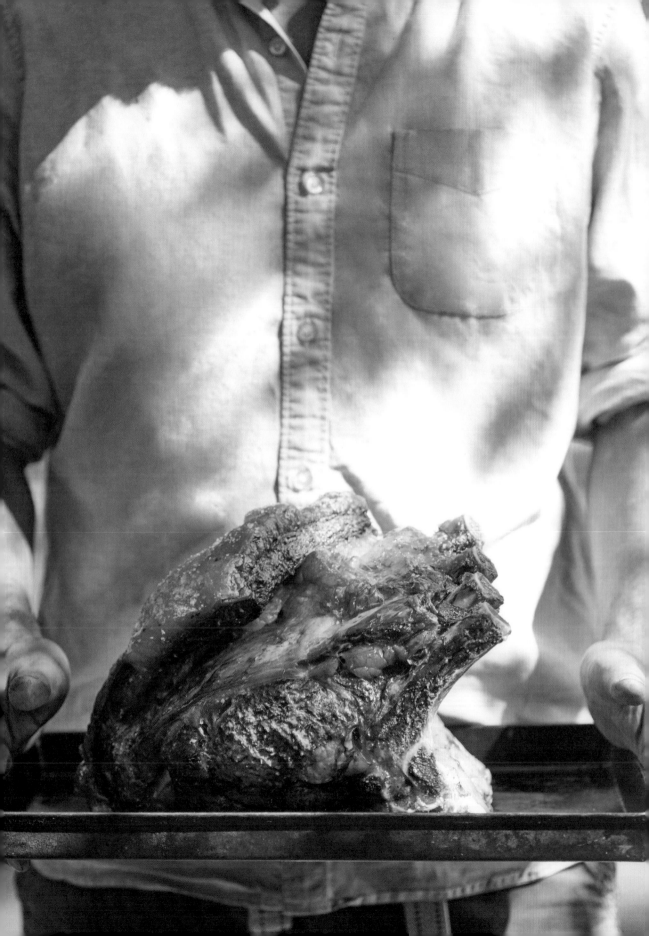

FRAGRANT SICHUAN SHORT RIBS

Short ribs are another BBQ classic you will want to master; pulling bones from a cooked rack and having them slide out clean is a moment of great satisfaction. The aim of this recipe isn't to test your patience, although it might do that with its 5–7-hour cooking time.

Here, you are managing a long cook with low temperature control and adding the wrapping element after a few hours. Wrapping helps keep the meat moist, preventing drying out and charring. As you get more experienced and better at temperature management, you may decide to not wrap at all. I suggest you do, though, for the first few cooks at least. Now... the peach-paper-versus-foil debate. It's not something we are going to waste our time on here. Using peach paper is favoured by the BBQ traditionalist. Using foil, known a little disparagingly as the 'Texas crutch', is fine, but it will speed the cooking up a little. If you have peach paper, use it, but if you don't, use foil.

SERVES 4

EGG SET UP
Indirect set-up; convEGGtor in legs-up position with the stainless-steel grill on top of the convEGGtor legs.

TARGET TEMP
125–135°C / 260–275°F

2kg / 4lb 6oz short ribs	**For the sauce**	2 thin slices of fresh ginger
1 tbsp flaky sea salt	80ml / ⅓ cup Chinese vinegar (or sherry vinegar)	2 star anise
2 tsp cracked black pepper		1 piece of cassia or cinnamon bark
1 tbsp dried chilli flakes	2 tbsp dark soy sauce	2 pieces of pared orange zest
1 tbsp ground Sichuan pepper	3 tbsp sugar	50ml / 3½ tbsp water
	4 garlic cloves, thinly sliced	

Mix the sauce ingredients together well and put to one side.

Season the ribs all over with the salt, black pepper, chilli flakes and Sichuan pepper, rubbing them in. If you have the time, let the ribs marinate overnight in the fridge (bringing them back to room temperature to cook), but at a minimum an hour or so before cooking.

Place the beef on the grill bone-side down, close the lid and cook for 3 hours, then remove and place on a double layer of peach paper or foil. Add the sauce then wrap up. Cook for another 2–4 hours until the internal temperature is 93–95°C / 200–203°F, then rest for 1 hour in a warm place. Strain the juices and skim off any excess fat before serving.

Accompany with rice noodles or steamed greens, with the strained sauce poured over the top.

COOK NO.11

EXPERT

SERVES 10+

EGG SET UP
Indirect set-up; convEGGtor in legs-up position with the stainless-steel grill on top of the convEGGtor legs.

Optional wood chips added to the charcoal.

TARGET TEMP
105–135°C / 220–275°F

PORK SHOULDER
with Vindaloo Spices

Few dishes are more misunderstood than vindaloo. It is an Indian derivation of a fairly simple Portuguese dish of pork in garlic and wine that has gained a reputation as a fiery curry-house staple. This recipe keeps the Indian flavours and complexity while dialling back the heat. Here you are dealing with a large piece of meat that needs looking after, basting every hour, while managing a long 'low and slow' cook. A transferable skill to all sorts of dishes. Remember, each time you open the EGG the temperature will fluctuate. Resist the temptation to fiddle with the vents and it will return to your target temperature.

2kg / 4lb 6oz pork shoulder

50g / 1¾oz salt

50g / 1¾oz sugar

For the vindaloo spice blend

1 tbsp ground black pepper

1 tbsp ground fennel seeds

2 tbsp Kashmiri chilli powder

2 tbsp garam masala

For the basting mix

150ml / ⅝ cup white wine vinegar or cider vinegar

100ml / generous ⅓ cup water

1 tbsp finely chopped garlic

1 tbsp finely grated ginger

2 tbsp sugar

2 tbsp vindaloo spice blend (see left)

For the sauce

1 red onion, chopped

2 garlic cloves, roughly chopped

1 tbsp finely grated fresh ginger

2–4 fresh chillies, finely chopped

½ tsp salt

2 tbsp vindaloo spice blend (see left)

50ml / 3½ tbsp basting mix (see left)

2 tbsp vegetable oil

100ml / generous ⅓ cup water

To serve

Salt and freshly ground black pepper

Quick pickled red onions (page 182)

Chopped coriander (cilantro)

Paratha (page 173) or soft tortillas (page 179), or serve with rice

Raita (page 187)

Zhug (page 190)

Mix the vindaloo spice blend ingredients together. Rub the pork with the salt, sugar and 2 tablespoons of the spice blend and allow to marinate at room temperature for an hour or so as it comes up to temperature. Combine the basting mix ingredients.

Place the pork fat side down on the grill, close the lid and cook for about 5 hours, brushing with the basting mix every hour or so. Wrap in peach paper or foil and cook for another 1–3 hours until the internal temperature reaches 92°C / 198°F. Rest for 10 minutes, then set aside, still wrapped, in a warm place for 1 hour.

To make the sauce, blitz everything except the oil and water to a paste in a blender. Heat the oil in a pan on the stove and cook the paste for 10 minutes or until the liquid has evaporated and the paste is frying, then add the water and cook to a thick sauce. Pull the meat with two forks, mix with the sauce and season with salt and pepper. Serve with pickled onions and chopped coriander in paratha or soft tortillas, with raita and zhug.

BRISKET

Here you are. BBQ rockstar status awaits...

What follows is a very basic brisket recipe. You can, once you have got the hang of it, experiment with rubs and marinades, but to start off, it's the classic salt and pepper. Briskets vary wildly depending on the breed of cattle, the feed, the age of the animal and butchery specifications, and all of these characteristics will affect how long it takes to cook. Which is why this isn't really a recipe, more a set of parameters.

Allow 1 hour of cooking time for each half kilo/pound of brisket, but this is just a guide. The truth is, I'm sorry to tell you, it's ready when it's ready. Furthermore, you will note there is no variation in the target temperature. Here you want to cook at 110°C/230°F until you reach an internal temperature of 75°C/167°F. At this point, wrap the meat, to prevent drying out and charring, and continue to cook until the internal temperature reaches 93°C/200°F.

1 brisket (beef point end brisket), 3–6kg/
6lb 10oz–13lb
Salt and freshly ground
black pepper

Cut any sinews from the brisket and remove the excess fat. Thoroughly rub the brisket with salt and pepper and let rest for at least 1 hour at room temperature.

Put the brisket on the grill fat side up, close the lid and calculate the cooking time as roughly an hour for each 0.5kg/1lb. Cook until the internal temperature reaches 75°C/167°F, then wrap in peach paper or foil and continue to cook until a core temperature of 93°C/200°F has been reached. The time may vary a lot.

Remove the brisket and rest it for at least 30 minutes before slicing.

COOK
NO.12

BBQ ROCKSTAR

SERVES 10+

EGG SET UP
Indirect set-up; convEGGtor in legs-up position with the stainless-steel grill on top of the convEGGtor legs.

Optional wood chips (hickory or oak) added to the charcoal.

TARGET TEMP
110°C/230°F

GRILLING

Grilling is the technique where the heat has direct contact with the thing you are cooking. Direct cooking, in other words. No convEGGtor or Dutch oven to regulate the temperature of, or protect, the food – it is what most people think of as BBQ-ing. The EGG is very efficient, but with direct cooking you do need to use quite a lot of charcoal to get the EGG hot and, in most cases, you won't be cooking for that long. Any remaining charcoal can be snuffed out and reused, or you can use that residual power from the EGG to cook something else – cooking and EGG efficiency combined. So in order to get the most out of my EGG and charcoal, I like combining cooks. If you are planning to grill for dinner, light the EGG early and make one of the Dutch oven dishes beforehand, then once that's done you can crank up the heat and grill your dinner. Alternatively, have one of the dishes from the Dirty and Afterburners chapter (page 102) prepped and ready to go.

Remember, you are controlling the temperature of your EGG here using the vents with the lid closed, only opening the EGG to place your ingredients inside, or to turn them. If you leave the lid open, you will lose control of the EGG's temperature and things can get tricky.

WHOLE TURBOT

SERVES 4–6

EGG SET UP
Direct set-up with the stainless-steel grill in place.

TARGET TEMP
150–180°C / 300–355°F

This recipe requires a fish cage – a traditional bit of kit that clamps around a fish, allowing you to grill and turn the fish over an open flame. I don't have one, so instead I rig together two wire cooling racks with some wire. Paperclips work well. Make sure the two racks are securely fastened around each edge and use tongs to grip the whole thing.

Prepare any sides before starting to cook the fish, and be ready to take it directly to the table, as the cooking will require constant attention.

My five-year-old son declared this the nicest thing he had ever eaten during its recipe testing. It is hard to disagree!

1 whole turbot or brill, 1.5–2kg / 3lb 5oz–4lb 6oz, gutted, trimmed and cleaned	75ml / 5 tbsp olive oil, plus extra for brushing	25ml / 1½ tbsp white wine vinegar
	50ml / 3½ tbsp fish stock	Sea salt
	25ml / 1½ tbsp white wine	

Dry the skin of the prepared fish, brush with oil, season with salt and place in a fish grilling cage (see above). Make the dressing by reducing the fish stock in a small pan on the stove by half, then whisking in the wine, vinegar and olive oil.

Place the turbot or brill in its cage on the grill, close the lid and cook for 5 minutes on each side, then brush with the dressing and continue to cook, turning it every 3–5 minutes and brushing with the dressing as you go, until it has an internal temperature of 55°C / 130°F or more in the thickest part of the fish, and the skin is charred and crispy. This should take about 20–30 minutes in total; see page 12 for how to 'burp' the EGG to open.

Gently remove the fish from the cage and either take off the bone by cutting down the backbone and gently lifting off the fillets, or I personally like to leave it whole and let everyone just attack it. Finish by spooning over any remaining dressing.

PAELLA
with Roasted Garlic Alioli

SERVES 10–12

EGG SET UP
Direct set-up with the
stainless-steel grill in place
and a paella pan on top.

TARGET TEMP
Around 180°C / 355°F

This might look like a complicated and difficult recipe, but trust
me, once you've got the hang of it, you'll knock it out in no time.
It is simply a fantastic thing to make and a fantastic way to eat
– a large pan in the centre of the table with everyone digging in.
Once you've got the method, play around with the flavours:
chorizo, snails, prawns, clams, mussels and squid all work well.

3 tbsp olive oil

2 chicken legs,
chopped into small
pieces through the bone
(about 12 pieces in total)

2 good-sized pork ribs,
chopped into small
pieces across the bone
(ask your butcher to
do this for you)

1 onion, finely diced

1 red (bell) pepper,
deseeded and finely
chopped

3 garlic cloves, finely
sliced

Generous pinch of
sweet paprika

3 canned plum
tomatoes, drained
of juice and roughly
chopped

Few strands of saffron,
soaked in a little warm
water for 10 minutes

800ml / 3⅓ cups hot
chicken stock or water

400g / 2 cups paella rice

125g / 1 cup fresh cooked
or frozen peas

1 x 400g / 14oz can
of butter (lima) beans,
rinsed and drained

Salt

Roasted garlic alioli
(page 183)

Lemon wedges, to serve

Add the oil to the heated paella pan, then add the chicken and the
pork ribs, close the lid of the EGG and brown for about 10 minutes
until nicely coloured, turning once halfway through.

Push the meat to the edges of the pan and add the onion, pepper
and garlic. Cook to soften for at least 5 minutes, then add the
paprika, tomatoes and saffron with its soaking water. Let the
mixture cook for about 5 minutes then stir the browned meat back
into the veg, mixing well with a wooden spoon.

Add the hot stock or water and bring to a fierce boil. Add salt to
taste (it should taste a bit saltier than you'd usually like, taking into
account the rice will absorb lots of flavour, about 1–1½ teaspoons
is good).

Add the rice, shaking the pan as you do, so that the mixture evens
out, and from now on don't stir – this will help with producing the
bottom crust ('socarrat') that makes for a good paella. Close the
lid and cook for about 20 minutes more, or until the rice is just
cooked and the liquid has been fully absorbed, scattering the peas
and butter beans over the surface of the paella once the liquid has
reduced by half (about 10 minutes).

Remove and rest the paella for at least 10 minutes. Meanwhile,
make the roasted garlic alioli. Serve the paella straight from the
pan, scraping up the bottom bits, with lemon wedges on the side to
squeeze and alioli to dollop over.

PRAWN SATAY

This is the most versatile of all the recipes in the book – the sauce will work with the traditional partnerships of prawn (shrimp), chicken and pork but equally well with goat, lamb, beef and tofu. Serve as a starter or with rice to make it a main meal. If using bamboo rather than metal skewers, soak them in water for 30 minutes.

1 tbsp sriracha sauce, plus extra to serve

4 tbsp kecap manis (or use light soy sauce mixed with 2 tsp sugar)

600g/1lb 5oz prawns (shrimp), or boneless meat of your choice, cut into small bite-sized pieces (about 2–3cm/ ¾–1¼in square)

1–2 tsp dried chilli flakes (as you prefer)

200ml/generous ¾ cup full-fat coconut milk

150g/⅔ cup peanut butter (no added sugar)

1 tsp ground turmeric

2 garlic cloves, finely chopped or crushed

1 tbsp finely grated or chopped fresh ginger

1 lime

Salt, if needed

1 or 2 cucumbers, peeled, deseeded and cut into batons, to serve

SERVES 4

EGG SET UP
Direct set-up with the stainless-steel grill in place.

TARGET TEMP
160–210°C/320–410°F

Mix the sriracha with half the kecap manis in a bowl or dish, add the prawns (or meat) and turn to coat, then cover and leave to marinate for as long as possible – throughout the day, overnight or for a couple of hours (refrigerate for longer times, bringing it back to room temperature to cook).

Whisk the remaining kecap manis with the chilli flakes and coconut milk in a small saucepan over a low heat on the stove. Add the peanut butter, turmeric, garlic and ginger then remove from the heat and blend the mix in a food processor or using a stick blender, along with the juice from half the lime. Check the seasoning and adjust, adding some salt and more chilli, if needed, and a little water if very thick. Put the sauce in a bowl and set aside to keep warm.

Thread the prawns onto skewers, place on the grill, close the lid and cook for a minute on each side (3–5 minutes on each side for meat) until the surface is nicely caramelized and the flesh is cooked through.

Serve the skewers and cucumber batons alongside the satay sauce for dipping, with the remaining lime half to squeeze, and more sriracha.

EGG SET UP
Direct set-up with the
stainless-steel grill in place.

TARGET TEMP
160–210°C / 320–410°F

BUTTERFLIED LEG OF LAMB
with Moscatel & Green Olives

Lamb and southern Spanish flavours combine here with the smoke to produce deep notes with a deliciously sharp finish. You could use butterflied shoulder here instead, or swap the lamb for goat.

1 leg of lamb, about 1.5kg / 3lb 5oz, boned and butterflied

50ml / 3½ tbsp good-quality extra-virgin olive oil (preferably Spanish)

50ml / 3½ tbsp moscatel vinegar (or use a mix of orange and lemon juice)

4 bay leaves, roughly chopped

3 garlic cloves, crushed

½ tsp sweet or bittersweet smoked paprika

2 tbsp fresh thyme leaves

½ tbsp each of salt and freshly ground black pepper

15 green olives, pitted and roughly chopped

Small bunch of parsley, leaves roughly chopped

½ tsp dried guindilla chilli flakes (or use mild chilli flakes)

Salt and freshly ground black pepper

In a dish large enough to hold the lamb, mix 1 tablespoon of the olive oil with half the vinegar, the bay leaves, garlic, paprika and half the thyme. Add the lamb, coat in the marinade, cover and place in the fridge overnight (or for at least 2 hours). Bring back to room temperature before cooking.

Season with the salt and pepper, then place the lamb on the grill, close the lid and cook for about 12–15 minutes on each side, turning often, or until nicely pink (cook more for more well-done meat).

Mix the olives with the remaining thyme, olive oil and vinegar, then stir through the parsley and the chilli flakes. Spoon the dressing over the lamb and rest for 10 minutes under foil, then slice to serve, testing for seasoning.

Serve with potatoes, sautéed or roasted with bell peppers, and a green salad.

GRILLED SQUID
with Nam Jim Jaew

This marinade and sauce works very well with prawns, most fish and even chicken. It is a quick cook, and whatever you do, don't overcook the squid. It needs to be cooked very quickly at a very high temperature. In and out, really fast. Make sure you preheat the grill.

SERVES 4–6

EGG SET UP
Direct set-up with the stainless-steel grill in place.

TARGET TEMP
200–240°C / 390–465°F

4 garlic cloves, finely chopped

½ small bunch of coriander (cilantro), stalks and leaves separated and finely chopped

2 lemongrass stalks, juicy lower part only, thinly sliced

80ml / ⅓ cup fish sauce

Juice of 1½ limes

¼ tsp finely ground white pepper

3–4 medium-large squid, cleaned

50g / scant ⅓ cup uncooked Thai sticky rice

20g / ¾oz red bird's-eye chillies, or another type of small, hot chilli

60g / 2oz palm sugar (or use light brown sugar)

1 large shallot, finely chopped

Mix the garlic, coriander stalks and lemongrass with half the fish sauce, the juice of ½ a lime, and the white pepper. Pour over the squid and marinate for at least 30 minutes and up to 4 hours.

Once your EGG has preheated, allow it to stand for another 30 minutes before you cook the squid. Heat a skillet in the EGG for 1 minute then add the rice in a single layer. Toast for 10–20 minutes, shaking often until the rice is lightly golden.

Allow the rice to cool for 5 minutes while you grill the chillies in a single layer for 5 minutes until charred and beginning to soften, then remove and allow to cool. Once cool enough to handle, finely chop (removing the seeds if you want it less hot). Grind the rice to a coarse powder in a pestle and mortar or spice grinder.

To make the nam jim jaew, mix the sugar with the remaining fish sauce, the juice of 1 lime, 1 tbsp of the toasted rice powder, the shallot and the chopped coriander leaves, then add the chopped roasted chilli to taste.

Remove the squid from the marinade, place on the grill, close the lid and cook for 1–3 minutes each side until just cooked. Serve sprinkled with a bit more rice powder and with the sauce on the side to dip.

GREEN TANDOORI CHICKEN

SERVES 4

EGG SET UP
Direct set-up with the stainless-steel grill in place.

TARGET TEMP
190–210°C / 375–410°F

This is a favourite in my house. The zingy lemon and coriander mingle with the charred, crispy bits for chicken perfection. You can scale up this marinade to use with a poussin or half chicken if you like.

8 chicken thighs, skin removed if you prefer

For the marinade
Small bunch of coriander (cilantro), about 15g / ½oz, roughly chopped

2 garlic cloves, roughly chopped

1–3 fresh green chillies, seeds removed if you want less heat, roughly chopped

1 tbsp grated fresh ginger

1 tsp ground turmeric

1 tbsp garam masala

1 tsp chilli powder, or more or less to taste

Juice of 1 lemon

1 tbsp sugar

1 tsp salt

½ tsp cracked black pepper

1 tbsp vegetable oil

To serve
Paratha or naan breads (pages 173 or 171)

Raita (page 187)

Zhug (page 190)

Blend the marinade ingredients together in a food processor and mix into the chicken to fully coat. Cover and allow to marinate for at least 1 hour, or up to 8 hours or overnight in the fridge (bringing them back to room temperature before cooking).

Remove the chicken from the marinade and thread evenly between four skewers. Place each skewer directly onto the grill, skin side down if you kept it on. Close the lid and grill for 10 minutes. Turn the chicken thighs and grill for another 10–15 minutes or until the internal temperature is 74°C / 165°F.

Rest for 10 minutes before serving with breads, raita and the zhug (or another chilli sauce). You can cook these without the skewers and serve on the bone, or pull and roughly shred the chicken, if you prefer.

QUICK GRILLED SHORT RIBS
or Sliced Pork Belly with Chimichurri

These ribs are cut in the 'flanken' style, meaning they are cut across the ribs, giving you a cross-section view, rather than lengthways, as is more common (make sure you do get the right cut or it won't work). It's a great way of getting to use this cut without having to wait hours for it to cook. This recipe works just as well with slices of pork belly, but they will take a minute longer on each side.

I love this recipe, as short ribs or pork belly usually require loads of time and effort, and this cuts right through all that. Quick, simple and delicious. Once you've mastered the basic cook, try adding your favourite rub or spice mix to the meat before cooking.

800g/1¾lb flanken-cut short ribs, about 2–3cm/¾–1¼in thick (see above), or use pork belly, removed from fridge before lighting the EGG

Flaky sea salt and coarsely ground black pepper

Chimichurri (page 190), or your favourite steak sauce, to serve

Season both sides of the ribs generously with the salt and pepper then place on the grill, close the lid and grill for 4–6 minutes on each side, to the desired doneness (it is best served medium-rare).

Allow to rest for 5 minutes before serving with sauce on the side.

SERVES 4

EGG SET UP
Direct set-up with the stainless-steel grill in place.

TARGET TEMP
190C–210°C / 375–410°F

EGG SET UP
Direct set-up with the
stainless-steel grill in place.
You'll need a skillet.

TARGET TEMP
230–250°C / 445–480°F

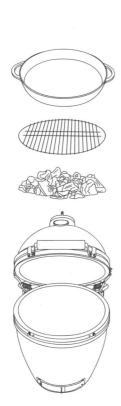

SEARED ONGLET À L'ÉCHALOTE

This is a classic French bistro dish. If you are trimming the onglet
yourself, remove the connective tissue between each section,
then trim away any excessive silver skin. Good onglet should have
the slightest hint of 'liveriness' to it.

800g / 1¾lb onglet
(hanger) or bavette
steak, trimmed weight,
removed from fridge
before lighting the EGG

1 tbsp olive oil

100g / scant ½ cup cold
butter, diced

400g / 14oz shallots,
peeled and thinly sliced

2 garlic cloves, finely
chopped

100ml / generous ⅓ cup
red wine

1 tbsp red wine vinegar

Salt and freshly cracked
black pepper

Coat the steak with the olive oil, season generously with salt and
pepper and allow to sit for 5 minutes.

Place a cast-iron skillet on the grill to preheat. Place the steak in
the skillet, close the lid and cook for 2–3 minutes on each side until
the internal temperature of the meat reaches about 50°C / 120°F.
Remove the steak from the skillet and leave to rest for 5–10 minutes
in a warm place.

Add 30g / 2 tbsp of the butter to the skillet along with the shallots
and garlic. Stir well, then cook for 3–4 minutes until the shallots are
softened and beginning to brown at the edge, giving the sauce a
stir once during cooking.

Add the steak back to the skillet, then add the remaining butter,
the wine and vinegar, close the EGG lid and cook for 2–3 minutes
until the liquid is almost evaporated, without allowing it to boil.

Cut the meat thinly across the grain and serve topped with the
butter and shallot sauce.

VERDURA MISTA

The literal translation from Italian is 'mixed vegetables', which is why chefs always call it verdura mista. It's much sexier. This works year round, so try mixing up your veg for each season, to get the best flavour out of them. Try and get the criss-cross pattern from the grill on the veg for extra prettiness. The grilled vegetables will absorb a lot of olive oil once cooked, so apply it liberally.

SERVES 4 AS A MAIN COURSE
or 8 as a side

EGG SET UP
Direct set-up with the stainless-steel grill (or cast-iron grid if you have one) in place.

TARGET TEMP
180–200°C / 355–390°F

In summer:

1 large aubergine (eggplant), sliced lengthways, 1cm/ ⅜in thick

2 courgettes (zucchini), sliced lengthways, 1cm/ ⅜in thick

Bunch of asparagus, about 350g/12¼oz

2 red (bell) peppers

2 yellow (bell) peppers

In winter:

1 fennel bulb, cut into 5mm/⅛in slices, leafy tops reserved

1 medium squash, cut into 4–5cm/1½–2in slices

2 red onions, cut into 2–3cm/¾–1¼in wedges

To serve

90ml/6 tbsp extra-virgin olive oil, plus extra to drizzle

3 tbsp red wine vinegar

2 garlic cloves, finely chopped

A good spoonful of smoked ricotta (page 99)

Small bunch of basil, leaves picked

Sea salt and freshly ground black pepper

Put all the vegetables onto a large tray, ready to cook. In batches, place the veg directly onto the grill, close the lid and cook for about 5–10 minutes, or until charred, soft and delicious. Remember that each vegetable will cook in a different amount of time, so keep checking and turning everything, and as soon as it is looking good, transfer it to a large bowl (keeping the cooked peppers, if using, to one side for now) and get the next lot of veg on.

If using, carefully remove the black skin on the peppers, open them up and scrape away the seeds. Don't worry about getting all of the skin off but do the best you can. This is a messy job but worth it. Tear the peppers up into strands and add to the bowl.

Mix together the olive oil, vinegar, garlic and a good pinch each of salt and pepper then toss through the cooked vegetables.

Arrange the vegetables on a large plate or in a bowl. Crumble over the smoked ricotta, tear the basil leaves over, scatter over the fennel tops (if using), and douse the lot in more olive oil.

BURNT CALÇOTS & ROMESCO

Every January the Catalans hold a 'Calçotada', a celebration of the calçot, a sort of spring onion-leek hybrid. Hundreds gather around open fires and picnic tables taking turns to peel off the charred casing, eating the calçots in one go in a method somewhere in between sword swallowing and a sea bird woofing down a fish.

They can be cooked dirty or as an 'afterburner', or direct, as here; the essential thing is to char the outer layer so the inner 'meat' steams to sweet, floppy perfection. Avoid thin calçots – they need to be at least as thick as your thumb. Smallish leeks would work as a replacement if you can't find calçots, with the tops trimmed off.

SERVES 4

EGG SET UP
Direct set-up with the stainless-steel grill in place.

TARGET TEMP
220–250°C / 430–480°F

2 bunches of fat calçots (about 15–20), or small leeks

For the Romesco
1 red (bell) pepper
1 head of garlic
1 large shallot
1 large tomato

1 large slice of sourdough or ciabatta bread
1 tbsp red wine vinegar or sherry vinegar, plus extra to taste
1 tsp paprika (smoked or unsmoked)
Pinch of dried chilli flakes (optional, to taste)

3 tbsp extra-virgin olive oil, plus extra for the calçots
50g / 1¾oz flaked (slivered) or whole almonds (or you can use hazelnuts)
Salt and freshly ground black pepper

For the Romesco, place the red pepper, garlic bulb, shallot and tomato on the grill, close the lid and roast for 12–15 minutes, turning them once, until soft.

Toast the bread, remove the crusts, and rip into small pieces. Peel the roasted shallot and pepper, removing the seeds from the pepper, and squeeze out the soft middles from the garlic.

Put the toasted bread, soft garlic, roasted peppers, shallot, tomato, vinegar, paprika and chilli flakes, if using, in a food processor and process until smooth. Add the olive oil in a thin stream until it is fully emulsified, then add the almonds and pulse to a very coarse sauce, with texture. Add salt and pepper to taste, plus more vinegar if you like, and put to one side.

Add the calçots to the grill, close the lid and roast for 6–8 minutes, turning a couple of times, until the outside is slightly charred and the middle is tender. Wrap the calçots in newspaper or foil and leave somewhere warm to rest for 10–15 minutes (this extra steaming makes the outer layer easy to remove).

Pinch or slice off the base of each calçot and peel away the charred outer leaves, then dip in the Romesco sauce to serve.

PLANCHA

A plancha is a flat metal plate heated for cooking, but in the context of an EGG you can also use a ceramic plate, skillet or cast-iron griddle or pan. The advantage of plancha-style cooking is that the evenness of the heat transferred though the metal confers an even cook onto the meat. You can also use it to get a lovely crisp skin on fish and poultry, and it's a great way of extending the cooking area of a lit EGG while you are direct cooking something else.

DUCK BREAST

Keeping the skin pressed down flat to the metal for the first 30 seconds of the cook will ensure an even, crispy skin on the duck. This recipe would work with a whole duck, in which case roast it at 180°C/355°F indirect, then increase to 250°C/480°F for about 45 minutes, glaze then return for 10–15 minutes.

SERVES 4

EGG SET UP
Direct set-up with the stainless-steel grill and plancha in place.

TARGET TEMP
180–200°C/355–390°F

4 duck breasts	**For the glaze**	1 tsp fresh thyme leaves
Salt and freshly ground black pepper	2 tbsp duck fat or olive oil	50g/1¾oz redcurrant jelly
	1 garlic clove, very finely chopped	1 tbsp Armagnac or brandy (or cider brandy/Calvados)

Pat the duck dry and season both sides with salt and pepper.

Add the duck breasts to the plancha, fat side down, and press down using a metal spatula for 30 seconds (this ensures evenly crisp skin; you could also use a brick, as in the chicken recipe on page 98). Close the lid and cook for 8–10 minutes until golden brown, then turn and cook for a further 8–10 minutes.

Meanwhile, mix the glaze ingredients together in a bowl.

Liberally brush the glaze over each side of the duck then let rest on a chopping board for 6–8 minutes before cutting into slices 2cm/¾in thick; you are looking for an internal temperature of 60–63°C/140–145°F for medium doneness. Serve immediately.

LAMB RACK
with Salsa Verde

This is a quick cook which you may want to combine with another. The calçots on page 91 would make a nice side dish, or maybe serve the scallops on page 114 as a starter, cooking them as the lamb racks are resting.

Salsa verde is incredibly versatile. It goes well with fish, chicken and roasted vegetables. You could even use a spoonful as a base of a salad dressing. It is extremely useful to have up your sleeve.

4 tbsp salsa verde (page 189), plus extra to serve

2 lamb racks

Spread the salsa verde over both sides of the lamb and allow to marinate for 1 hour.

Lay each rack on the plancha, close the lid and sear on each side for 4 minutes. Remove the lamb and put to one side while you add in the convEGGtor to switch to indirect cooking.

Once the grill is set up and the temperature has dropped to 190°C/375°F, which should only take 3–4 minutes, place the lamb on the grill, bones pointing up, interlocking each bone so the racks support one another. Close the lid and cook for 20–30 minutes until the internal temperature reads 53°C/127°F.

Allow to rest for a minimum of 10 minutes on a chopping board, before carving into cutlets/chops and serving with a little more salsa verde.

SERVES 2

EGG SET UP
Direct set-up with the stainless-steel grill and plancha in place, then indirect set-up with the convEGGtor in legs-up position, with the stainless-steel grill on top of the convEGGtor legs.

TARGET TEMP
210–230°C/340–445°F, then 190°C/375°F

MACKEREL
with Fennel Dressing

SERVES 6

EGG SET UP
Marinate the fish before lighting the EGG.

Direct set-up with the stainless-steel grill and plancha in place (or cast-iron grid if you have one).

TARGET TEMP
160–190°C / 285–375°F

Fresh mackerel are hard to beat but this recipe will work with sardines, trout or herring, too. When you lay them on the plancha, line them up with enough room so you can roll them over with a spoon, spatula or fish slice, using the spine as the pivot point. This will give you the best chance of keeping them in one piece and not breaking the skin.

2 fennel bulbs, trimmed and finely chopped (including any fronds)

2 large shallots, very finely chopped

2 garlic cloves, very finely chopped

2 tbsp capers, roughly chopped

Bunch of flat-leaf parsley, leaves finely chopped

Juice and finely grated zest of 2 lemons

2 tbsp Chardonnay vinegar or other white wine vinegar

150ml / ⅝ cup olive oil, plus extra for the fish

6 medium-sized fresh mackerel, cleaned and gutted

Salt and freshly ground black pepper

Mix the fennel and shallots in a bowl, stir in 1 teaspoon of salt and leave for 20 minutes, then rinse and drain.

Add the garlic, capers, parsley, lemon zest and juice, vinegar and olive oil to the fennel and shallot mixture, adding salt and pepper to taste.

Make 5–6 deep slashes in either side of each fish and season generously inside and out with salt and pepper, then rub in 4 tablespoons of the fennel mixture, getting some inside the belly cavity. Allow to marinate for at least 15 minutes.

Lightly oil the outside of the fish then place them on the grill and close the lid. Cook for 7–8 minutes, then carefully turn the fish over and cook for another 7–8 minutes, or until the meat is opaque and can lift away from the bone.

Serve the fish with the remaining fennel mixture on the side.

EGG SET UP
Direct set-up with the stainless-steel grill and plancha in place.

TARGET TEMP
160–180°C / 320–355°F

BRICK
CHICKEN THIGHS
with Harissa

You'll need a couple of bricks wrapped in foil for this. Failing that you can use a cast-iron skillet, or a special grill press if you have one. Either way, you want something quite heavy.

There are two different marinades here. They are both great and work best if on the chicken for at least 2 hours before cooking, but, as is nearly always the case, overnight is best. Alternatively, cook the chicken simply with olive oil, salt and pepper.

This can also be made with a whole boned chicken, just add 5–6 minutes of cooking time and turn it a few times to be sure it is cooked through.

	Marinade 1	Marinade 2
12 boneless, skin-on chicken thighs (ask your butcher to bone them out)	1 tsp dried chilli flakes	2 tsp toasted and ground cumin seeds
Salt	4 garlic cloves	2 tsp toasted and ground coriander seeds
1 quantity harissa (page 186), to serve	Grated zest of 1 lemon	½ tsp ground cardamom
	1 tbsp fresh thyme leaves, or roughly chopped rosemary needles	1 tsp ground cinnamon
	2 tbsp olive oil	2 garlic cloves
		1 small onion, roughly chopped
		2 tbsp olive oil

Combine the ingredients for whichever marinade you are using in a food processor and whiz to a paste, or just finely chop the dry ingredients together using a heavy knife on a chopping board, then mix in the olive oil.

In a bowl or dish, rub the marinade all over the chicken, then cover and put in the fridge for 2 hours or overnight to marinate, bringing it back to room temperature before cooking.

Season the chicken with salt and lay on the plancha skin side down. Close the lid and cook for a couple of minutes to set the skin, then place the foiled bricks on top of the chicken, pressing in an even layer under the weight. Cook for 6–10 minutes until the meat is cooked through.

Let the chicken rest for 5 minutes before slicing into strips – or keep whole if you'd rather – then serve with harissa on the side.

SMOKED RICOTTA

Smoky, roasted ricotta makes a brilliant addition to any of the grilled or baked recipes in this book, and it's also a lovely lunch on good toast. It would work as an 'afterburner' after a hot-temperature cook – just leave the cheese in the EGG until it's completely cooled. The recipe here is for one ricotta, but you can scale up the quantities to make more.

250g/9oz ricotta in a single piece, drained

2 tbsp finely chopped fresh herbs (any mixture of flat-leaf parsley, thyme, chives and basil)

Pinch of dried chilli flakes (optional)

30ml/2 tbsp extra-virgin olive oil

½ tsp cracked coriander seeds or fennel seeds

Flaky sea salt and freshly ground black pepper

Season the ricotta with salt and pepper and place on the plancha (or in a preheated frying pan). Close the lid and cook for 25–30 minutes or until light brown.

Meanwhile, combine the chopped herbs, chilli flakes (if using) and olive oil and season with salt and pepper. Five minutes before the ricotta is ready, spoon over 1 tablespoon of the herb mixture and sprinkle with the spice seeds.

Remove the ricotta to a plate and top with the remaining herb mixture to serve.

MAKES 1

EGG SET UP
Direct set-up with the stainless-steel grill and plancha in place.

TARGET TEMP
170–200°C/340–390°F

OX HEART PINCHOS MORUNOS

SERVES 2

EGG SET UP
Direct set-up with the stainless-steel grill and plancha in place.

TARGET TEMP
230–250°C / 445–480°F

These flavours are inspired by Moorish cuisine in Spain, and are popular in Andalusia and Extremadura; however, ox heart is a popular skewer in Peru, called anticuchos. If you are a bit wary of heart, I urge you to try it – it is just a muscle and cooks like steak, and doesn't have any of the offal flavour associated with liver or kidneys.

600–800g / 1lb 5oz–1lb 12oz ox heart, cut into 3–4cm / 1¼–1½in cubes

Salt and freshly ground black pepper

For the marinade

1 tbsp olive oil

1 tsp hot or sweet pimentón (Spanish paprika)

1 tsp ground cumin

1 tsp dried oregano

½ tsp ground fennel seeds

1 garlic clove, crushed

In a bowl or dish, mix together all the ingredients for the marinade, add the meat, then turn to coat and marinate for at least an hour; anything up to 24 hours is fine (in the fridge), as the meat will just take on more flavour. Bring to room temperature before cooking.

Thread the marinated meat onto metal skewers and season with salt and pepper.

Add to the plancha, close the lid and cook for 2–3 minutes on each side – you want the cubes to be just cooked through and still juicy on the inside, although they can be cooked as pink as you like.

Serve on paratha (page 173) or even with the calçots on page 91.

SALT & PEPPER PRAWNS

Finger bowls, complete with slices of lemon, are a must. Cooking the prawns with the shell on improves their flavour and will help protect the flesh from overcooking. There is also plenty of flavour in the heads.

1 tbsp ground Sichuan pepper (or more or less to taste)

2 tsp cracked black pepper (or more or less to taste)

2 tsp dried chilli flakes (or more or less to taste)

Good pinch of salt (coarse or flaky is good here)

1kg/2lb 2oz large shell-on prawns (shrimp), with or without heads

50ml/3½ tbsp vegetable oil

3 garlic cloves, thinly sliced

4 spring onions (scallions), thinly sliced

Combine the Sichuan pepper, black pepper, chilli flakes and salt. You might prefer more of the numbing heat of the Sichuan pepper or more heat from the chilli. Keep to one side.

Toss the prawns in 2 teaspoons of the spice mixture. Shake off any excess and lay them out on a tray, not touching each other (this can be done ahead).

When ready to cook, heat the oil in a frying pan on the stove until hot. You can test the temperature by frying a small piece of garlic – it should sizzle instantly and turn golden in about 30 seconds. Add all the sliced garlic and cook for about 30 seconds until golden, then remove from the heat and set aside.

Add the coated prawns to the plancha, close the lid and grill for 1–2 minutes or until golden crisp and just cooked through. Remove to a platter, sprinkle with more of the spice mixture and the spring onions, and drizzle with your garlic oil. Serve with finger bowls and napkins.

SERVES 4

EGG SET UP
Direct set-up with the stainless-steel grill and plancha in place.

TARGET TEMP
250–300°C / 480–570°F

DIRTY AND AFTERBURNERS

Dirty and afterburner cooking are, for me, predominantly ways of extending the life of your charcoal. 'Dirty' cooking is the BBQ term for putting the thing you are cooking directly on the lit charcoal. It gives an intense, elemental flavour to the food but requires great care. Only start cooking dirty once you are confident in your ability to manage the EGG.

'Afterburners' apply when you are finished with your cook, closing down your EGG and you want to make use of the heat in the charcoal. Rarely do I let the EGG cool down without something sitting on the grill, or in the charcoal, for another time.

STEAK ON COALS

The steak fat directly on the charcoal will smoke a lot, so don't worry when it starts. Dirty cooking will work with any steak, but they must be thick-cut.

SERVES 1

EGG SET UP
Direct set-up with no surfaces in place.

TARGET TEMP
250–300°C / 480–570°F

1 steak, cut 4cm / 1½in thick, removed from fridge before lighting the EGG

Olive oil

Flaky sea salt and coarsely ground black pepper

Allow the charcoal to get hot over the area that you will need to cook the steaks. You're looking for charcoal that is glowing or white.

Season the steak generously with salt and rub in a little oil. Place directly onto the charcoal and close the lid (there will be a lot of smoke).

Cook for 3 minutes, then turn and cook for another 3 minutes.

Remove the steak and wipe off any charcoal bits, then add a generous grind of black pepper. Allow to rest for at least 5 minutes before serving. If you like, place a scoop of anchovy butter (page 191) on the steak to melt as the steak is resting.

HISPI CABBAGE
with Jalapeño Buttermilk & Ancho Dressing

SERVES 4 AS A SIDE

EGG SET UP
Direct set-up with no surfaces in place.

TARGET TEMP
180–210°C / 355–410°F

As you are going to the effort of making the ancho chilli dressing, I suggest making loads. It keeps very well.

1 large green hispi cabbage, about 1kg / 2lb 2oz

200ml / generous ¾ cup olive oil, plus extra for rubbing

1 banana shallot, unpeeled

4 garlic cloves, unpeeled

6 ancho or pasilla chillies, de-stemmed and deseeded

75ml / 5 tbsp red wine vinegar

2 jalapeño chillies, halved lengthways

150ml / ⅝ cup buttermilk

Small bunch of coriander (cilantro), roughly chopped

1 tsp ground cumin

Juice of 1 lime

Salt and freshly ground black pepper

Pumpkin seeds, to serve

Rub the cabbage lightly with olive oil and season generously with salt, ensuring that all sides are well coated. Make a well in the centre of the coals using a tool, and carefully add the cabbage, then bury the cabbage completely by covering it with the surrounding hot coals. You can grill something on top at the same time if desired. Close the lid and maintain the temperature at about 200°C / 390°F.

The cabbage should be completely charred and black on all sides and tender in the centre after about 10 minutes. Check by piercing with a cake tester or paring knife. If it's not done, continue roasting in the coals for 5 more minutes. If you are preparing the cabbage ahead, wrap tightly in foil once cooked.

Add the shallot, three of the garlic cloves and the ancho or pasilla chillies to the coals for 5 minutes until fragrant, then peel the shallot and garlic and pulse very briefly in a blender. Stir through the olive oil and vinegar, adding salt to taste, and put to one side.

Roast the jalapeños skin side down on the coals for 5 minutes, then scrape off any black skin, remove the seeds and roughly chop. Blend the jalapeño with the buttermilk, half the coriander, the remaining garlic, the cumin, lime juice and salt and pepper to taste.

Cut the cabbage through the core into quarters and remove the core from each piece. Spoon the jalapeño dressing onto a serving platter, arrange the cabbage wedges on top and season lightly with salt, then spoon over the ancho dressing. Sprinkle over the pumpkin seeds and remaining coriander to serve.

ASH-COOKED SAUSAGE

with Shallot, Red Wine, Garlic & Thyme

For a variation you could cook the same recipe with chorizo in red wine, or even in cider.

8 large sausages

250ml/1 cup light, acidic red wine, such as a Pinot Noir, Dolcetto or Gamay

2 large shallots, thinly sliced

3 garlic cloves, thinly sliced

1 sprig of thyme

Salt and freshly ground black pepper

Make two foil packets, each made with three layers of foil and large enough to hold 4 sausages each. Prick the sausages with a fork and place 4 in each package, then divide the wine, shallots, garlic and thyme between the packets. Season with salt and pepper to taste and seal the packets securely.

Make a well in the centre of the coals using a tool, then carefully add the packets and bury completely by covering them with the surrounding hot coals. Close the lid and cook for 25–30 minutes. Remove the packets and carefully unfurl, taking care not to spill any of the juices.

Remove the sausages to a board and slice. Place on warm plates and pour the juices over the top. Serve with the baked potatoes on page 146.

Serve with the baked potatoes on page 146.

SERVES 4

EGG SET UP
Direct set-up with no surfaces in place (although this is suited to afterburning cooking on whatever set-up you have).

TARGET TEMP
150–300°C / 300–570°F

ESCALIVADA

This is a traditional Catalan dish of smoky grilled vegetables. The name comes from the Catalan verb escalivar, 'to cook in ashes' – referencing its traditional preparation in the embers of the wood fire. The smokiness imparted by cooking in this manner is essential to the flavour of the dish. This also works with the vegetables cooked on the grill.

SERVES 4 AS A SIDE
or by itself with garlic-rubbed toast, or with eggs

EGG SET UP
Direct set-up with no surfaces in place.

TARGET TEMP
180–210°C / 355–410°F

3 red (bell) peppers

2 aubergines (eggplant)

5 large, ripe tomatoes

3 tbsp extra-virgin olive oil, plus extra to serve

3 garlic cloves, very finely chopped

A little good-quality red wine vinegar or sherry vinegar

Salt and freshly ground black pepper

1 small can of good-quality anchovy fillets, to serve (optional)

Set the peppers, aubergines and tomatoes in the coal embers, then close the lid and cook, turning every now and then until the skins are charred and the veg is soft. The aubergines should take a fair bit longer; they want to be completely collapsed.

When the veg is cooked, remove and leave until cool enough to handle, then remove and discard the skins, and the pepper seeds. Roughly chop the flesh and combine with the olive oil and garlic. Season to taste with salt, pepper and vinegar. Serve at room temperature, drizzling with a bit more olive oil, with the anchovy fillets over the top, if using.

LEEKS VINAIGRETTE

This was a regular on the Great Queen Street menu when I was a full-time chef what feels like a million years ago, although we used to roast the leeks in the oven so they didn't get that smoky hit that really elevates the leek above the sum of its parts. It makes a great lunch or side to fish, and would work particularly well with the Turbot on page 78 or the brined chicken on page 62.

10 leeks

2 eggs, hard-boiled and coarsely grated

1 tbsp capers

Small bunch of flat-leaf parsley, dill or tarragon, leaves finely chopped

Salt and freshly ground black pepper

For the vinaigrette

2 tsp Dijon mustard

2 tbsp crème fraîche

1 tbsp white wine vinegar or cider vinegar

5 tbsp extra-virgin olive oil

SERVES 4–6 AS A SIDE

EGG SET UP
Direct set-up with no surfaces in place (but it will also work with the grill in place).

TARGET TEMP
180–210°C / 355–410°F

Check that the leeks are thoroughly clean and free of grit, then place in the embers, close the lid and cook for 20–30 minutes until the outsides are charred and the leeks are softened. Remove from the EGG and leave until cool enough to handle.

For the vinaigrette, put the mustard, crème fraîche and vinegar into a small bowl, add a little salt and pepper and whisk together. Whisk in the oil in a thin stream to emulsify.

Cut the root ends off the leeks, then run a sharp knife down the length of the leeks. Peel away the blackened layers and remove the soft middles. Roughly chop, place on warmed plates and season to taste with salt and pepper.

Spoon over half of the dressing, then the grated egg, capers and herbs, followed by the remaining dressing.

SERVES 8

EGG SET UP
Direct set-up with no surfaces in place; or indirect set-up, convEGGtor in legs-up position with the stainless-steel grill on top of the convEGGtor legs.

TARGET TEMP
180–210°C / 355–410°F

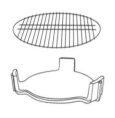

MIGAS-STUFFED WHOLE ONIONS

This works best if you throw the onions and garlic in the ashes after a low and slow cook, then come back to them the following day to squeeze them out and make the filling. They can, however, be made in one go.

8 medium onions, bottom root trimmed, top 1cm / ⅜in sliced off

3 heads of garlic

3 slices of sourdough or ciabatta bread

Small bunch of flat-leaf parsley, leaves finely chopped

30ml / 2 tbsp olive oil

2 chorizo or morcilla sausages, finely chopped

Salt and freshly ground black pepper

Place the onions and garlic in the embers (or on the grill), close the lid and bake for 30 minutes until completely soft.

While the garlic and onion are cooking, grill the bread for 3 minutes each side (if using the grill) until lightly toasted, then rip into small pieces and put to one side.

When the onion and garlic are soft, squeeze out the garlic flesh, mash it and mix into the bread. Squeeze out all of the onion flesh, leaving about 3 or 4 layers of onion in place to form a shell. Finely chop the onion flesh and put the reserved onion shells to one side.

Mix the chopped onion flesh, parsley, olive oil and chopped chorizo or morcilla into the garlicky bread, adding salt and pepper to taste. Spoon the mixture back into the reserved onion shells. (At this stage they can be placed in the fridge to cook the following day.) Place back in the EGG, either in the embers or on the grill, at about 160–200°C / 320–390°F, close the lid and cook for 15–20 minutes until hot throughout.

BURNT AUBERGINE, MISO & BLACK SESAME DIP

This is a version of the Japanese dish nasu dengaku. Like its Turkish cousin, imam bayildi, the aubergines are usually grilled, the innards scooped out, flavoured and replaced in the 'shells'. Here I've cooked the aubergines in their skins so they absorb all the smoky flavour.

SERVES 4

EGG SET UP
Direct set-up with the stainless-steel grill in place (although this is suited to afterburning cooking on whatever set-up you have).

TARGET TEMP
150–300°C / 300–570°F

4 large aubergines (eggplant), about 650g/1lb 7oz in total

3 tbsp mirin

3 tbsp sake or sweet sherry

3 tbsp white miso

2 tbsp rice wine vinegar

1–1½ tsp sugar

1 tsp grated fresh ginger

1 garlic clove, very finely chopped or crushed to a paste

½ bunch of spring onions (scallions), thinly sliced

2 tsp toasted black sesame seeds (or shichimi togarashi)

Salt and freshly ground black pepper

Put the aubergines on the grill or whatever set-up you have in place, close the lid and roast until completely charred and collapsed. Remove and allow to cool.

Slit the aubergines lengthways and scoop out the flesh in long strands, discarding the skins (it doesn't matter if the odd bit of skin gets in), then roughly chop.

In a serving bowl, stir the mirin and sake into the miso until it loosens up. Add the aubergines along with the vinegar, sugar, ginger and garlic. Season to taste, checking the vinegar and sugar; you want these flavours to balance.

Top with the spring onions and sesame seeds, and serve.

EGG SET UP
Direct set-up with the
stainless-steel grill in place,
or no surfaces in place.

TARGET TEMP
200–250°C / 390°F–480°F

SCALLOPS IN SHELL
with Hazelnut & Herb butter

This may be my favourite afterburner. It works really well as a
starter, cooked after the main course is done and is resting. Have
everything ready to go, in the fridge. Be vigilant; scallops don't
take long and it is easy to overcook them, and take care lifting the
scallops out – dripping liquid butter onto the charcoal will cause
flare-ups.

Simon Stullard, who runs the Hidden Hut in Cornwall in the UK,
finishes this dish by spraying Champagne from the bottle, like
a winning racing car driver, over the scallops. It's an impressive
sight and if you fancy showing off a little you could give it a try...

Small bunch of herbs,
such as flat-leaf parsley,
tarragon, chives or
thyme, finely chopped

30g / ¼ cup skinned
hazelnuts, toasted
and roughly chopped
or crushed

60g / 4½ tbsp softened
butter

Finely grated zest and
juice of 1 lemon

12 scallops in shell

1 tbsp capers, roughly
chopped

1 small shallot, very
finely chopped

Salt and freshly ground
black pepper

Crusty bread, to serve

Mix the herbs and hazelnuts into the softened butter along with
1 teaspoon of lemon zest, a squeeze of lemon juice and salt and
pepper to taste.

If your scallops need preparing, carefully prise open the shells with
a small knife, release the scallop from the shell with the knife
and discard the muscle, skirt and black stomach sack. Rinse the
scallops to remove any grit, pat them dry then place each scallop
back in a half-shell with 1 tablespoon of the flavoured butter, and
divide the capers and shallots between them.

Put the shells on the grill, or directly onto the coals, close the lid
and cook for 3–5 minutes, until the butter is bubbling and the
scallops are lightly cooked.

Serve topped with an extra squeeze of lemon juice and bread to
mop up the juices.

TRIPLE TOMATO SALAD:
Slow Roast, Raw & Dressing

This salad is great as a lunch with some good bread, or as a side dish for fish or chicken. A little cheese crumbled on the top is a nice variation. The smoked ricotta from page 99 would be perfect, but feta is good too.

600g/1lb 5oz ripe tomatoes

3 tbsp olive oil

1 small garlic clove, finely chopped

2 tbsp red wine vinegar or Chardonnay vinegar

2 sprigs of oregano or basil, leaves finely shredded

400g/14oz cherry tomatoes (a mixture of colours can be nice)

Flaky sea salt and freshly ground black pepper

Cut the tomatoes in half (not the cherry tomatoes) and season generously with salt.

Once you have finished cooking on your EGG, place the halved tomatoes cut side up on the grill, close the lid, snuff it out by closing both vents, and leave to slow-roast for 8 hours or until the following morning.

About 30 minutes before serving, chop and blend 100g/3½oz of the slow roast tomatoes with the olive oil, garlic and vinegar, then season to taste with salt and pepper and fold through the oregano or basil.

Chop the cherry tomatoes and lay them on a plate with the remaining cooked tomatoes, then coat with the dressing and serve.

SERVES 4

EGG SET UP
Direct set-up with the stainless-steel grill in place.

TARGET TEMP
200–220°C / 390–430°F

LOW AND SLOW

Low and Slow is where the EGG really comes into its own. The key message here is that temperature is your metric, not time. The timings I have given in the recipes are guides but the internal temperatures are not, and need to be adhered to. It is my experience that the problems one finds in low and slow recipes come from the 'slow' bit. The 'low' bit is easy to manage, and by the time you get cooking these you will be able to manage the EGG, I hope. The timing of things so everyone isn't sitting around until midnight waiting for dinner is the skill. Give yourself some slack at the other end. The meat can always rest while you gather everyone together.

WHOLE ROAST KID

Anissa Helou, in her fantastic book *Feast*, has a lovely Emirati recipe for whole roast kid called madfun. The recipe is as good as the name, with its collection of aromatic spices in the marinade. Here I go for something a little simpler, and if it is your first time cooking a whole beast I suggest you do the same. The flavour and texture of the meat after a long slow cook are out of this world (you are letting the EGG slowly smoke the meat until it falls off the bone) and you can play with the flavours next time. This is up there with the brisket as the best way to feed a crowd. You'll need a small kid – one that's about 3 months old.

This dish will be familiar to anyone who's eaten kid in Greece, southern Spain or Italy. The kid will form the centrepiece of a larger spread so you will want lots of condiments, sauces and side dishes on the table too. I suggest the masa harina soft tortillas on page 179, the corn on page 148, the chimichurri on page 190 and charred salsa on page 188, and even the mole from page 162 (but there is no reason to stop there!).

1 kid goat (or lamb),
about 10kg/22lb,
removed from fridge
before lighting the EGG

Salt and freshly ground
black pepper

Season the kid with salt and pepper and rub thoroughly into the meat.

Lay the kid on the grill, close the lid and cook for 6–8 hours or until you have an internal temperature (measure in the thick part of the leg) of 90°C/194°F.

Carefully remove from the EGG, wrap or cover with foil and rest for 30 minutes before serving.

SERVES A CROWD

EGG SET UP
Indirect set-up; convEGGtor in legs-up position with the stainless-steel grill on top of the convEGGtor legs, plus EGGspander if you have one.

TARGET TEMP
110°C–130°C/230–265°F

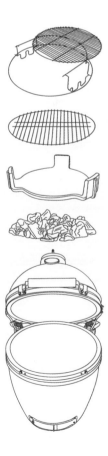

PORK OR OX CHEEKS
with Masa Harina Soft Tortilla

The sticky, gelatinous nature of the cheeks makes this a special recipe. Do go to the effort of making the masa harina soft tortillas; the earthiness of the masa adds another layer of flavour and it's a fun thing to do. You could add pecan smoking chips to the lit charcoal if you want.

1 tsp ground cumin

¼ tsp ground allspice

¼ tsp ground cinnamon

Pinch of ground cloves

1 tbsp ground ancho or pasilla chilli (or use sweet paprika)

1 tsp ground chipotle (or use hot smoked paprika)

1kg/2lb 2oz pork or ox cheeks, each cut into 4 pieces

1 small onion, root trimmed off

1 tbsp lard or dripping (or use vegetable oil)

1 whole ancho, pasilla or guajillo chilli, de-stemmed and deseeded

1 tbsp pumpkin seeds

4 garlic cloves, thinly sliced

Juice of 1 orange

2 ripe tomatoes, roughly chopped

1 tsp red or white wine vinegar

1 tsp sugar or honey

2 bay leaves (or avocado leaves)

Salt and freshly ground black pepper

To serve

Masa harina soft tortillas (page 179)

Quick pickled red onion (page 182)

Charred salsa (page 188)

Hot sauce

SERVES 4–6

EGG SET UP
Indirect set-up; convEGGtor in legs-up position with the stainless-steel grill on top of the convEGGtor legs. You'll need a Dutch oven.

TARGET TEMP
120–140°C/250–285°F

Mix the ground spices together in a small bowl, then rub half of them, along with 1 teaspoon of salt, into to the cheeks and marinate for 1 hour, or overnight in the fridge (bringing them to room temperature before cooking).

Place the cheeks and onion on the grill, close the lid and cook for 1–1½ hours until the cheeks are coloured and the onion is soft.

Place the remaining ingredients, including the remaining spice mixture, in a cast-iron pot and put into the EGG for 20 minutes towards the end of the cheeks' cooking time. Peel the cooked onion and blend to a coarse purée.

Once the cheeks are coloured, add them to the pot along with the onion purée and enough water to almost cover the cheeks. Close the lid and cook for about 1–1½ hours until the cheeks are tender and falling apart (the internal temperature should be about 95°C/203°F), topping up with water if it starts to dry out.

Remove from the EGG, remove the bay leaves and cheeks and put to one side. Blend the contents of the pot to a smooth sauce, adding a drop of water if needed, as well as salt and pepper to taste.

Return the cheeks to the pot, cover and rest for 20 minutes, then pull the meat into large shreds and stir through the sauce to coat. While the meat is resting, use the EGG to heat through the tortillas. Top the tortillas with shredded meat, pickled red onion, charred salsa and hot sauce.

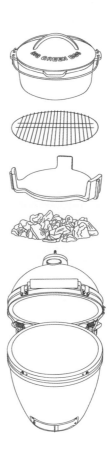

HERBED SIDE OF SALMON
or Sea Trout

SERVES 4–6

EGG SET UP
Marinate the fish before lighting the EGG.

Indirect set-up; convEGGtor in legs-up position with the stainless-steel grill on top of the convEGGtor legs.

TARGET TEMP
90–110°C / 194–230°F

If it will fit, the side can be cooked whole. If it won't, just cut it in half. The thinner edges will be a little more cooked than the middle, so share out different sections when serving. This is a wonderful summer centrepiece.

1 side of salmon, centre cut (the thickest section), or a large trout fillet (about 600g / 1lb 5oz)

Extra-virgin olive oil, for brushing

Salt and freshly ground black pepper

2 large shallots, finely chopped

Finely grated zest and juice of 1 lemon

A couple of small bunches of herbs (tarragon, chervil, chives or flat-leaf parsley), leaves and stalks separated and roughly chopped

Brush the salmon fillet all over with a little olive oil and lay on a baking tray. Season generously with salt and pepper, then top with the shallots, lemon zest and the chopped herb stalks.

Place the tray on the grill, close the lid and bake the salmon for about 30–40 minutes. You can tell it is done when the fish feels just firm to the touch and the white juices are just starting to break through the surface. You can rest it for 10 minutes then serve right away, or let it rest, covered in foil, for up to 2 hours before serving.

Gently brush the herbs and shallots off the salmon and add a squeeze of lemon juice, keeping the remaining lemon to serve as wedges at the table. Pull the salmon into big flakes and put onto a big platter or onto plates, topped with the chopped herb leaves.

Serve with a salad of raw vegetables and leaves, grilled vegetables, or the baked whole beetroot on page 151.

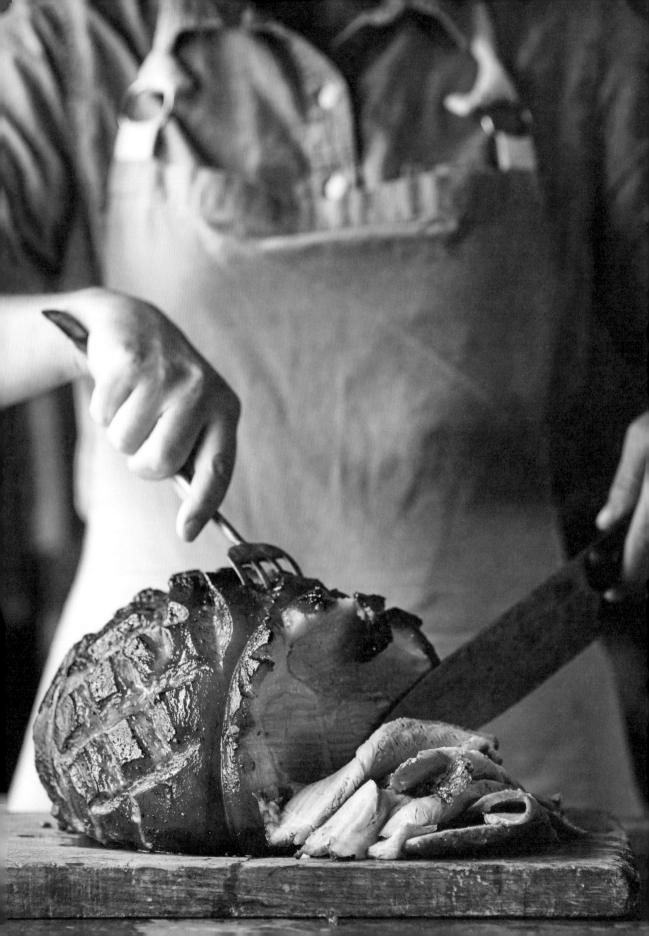

WHOLE HAM
with Spiced Port Glaze

Smoked ham is traditional at Christmas, and doing your own rather than buying them is extremely satisfying, but why deny yourself the rest of the year?

This is another cook where you can add smoking chips if you wish, but after 4 to 6 hours the smoke from the charcoal is usually enough.

1 unsmoked ham, about 4–5kg/8¾–11lb, skin scored with a sharp knife	**For the glaze**	50g/3 tbsp honey
	1 tbsp curry powder	250ml/1 cup red wine
	1 tbsp ground mixed spice	50ml/3½ tbsp Port
Olive oil	2 tbsp English mustard	50ml/3½ tbsp brandy or Port
	100g/½ cup brown sugar	Juice of 1 orange

Lightly oil the ham then place it on the grill with the scored skin facing down and close the lid.

Mix all the ingredients for the glaze in a bowl and put aside until later. After 2 hours, start brushing the ham with the glaze every 20 minutes until it begins to caramelize on the outside.

After 3½ hours, check the internal temperature, and when it has reached 72°C/161°F remove the ham from the EGG and rest for at least 30 minutes before carving. The overall cooking time will work out at about 1 hour per 1kg/2lb.

SERVES 12
with leftovers

EGG SET UP
Indirect set-up; convEGGtor in legs-up position with the stainless-steel grill on top of the convEGGtor legs.

TARGET TEMP
110–130°C/230–265°F

EGG SET UP
Indirect set-up; convEGGtor in legs-up position with the stainless-steel grill on top of the convEGGtor legs.

TARGET TEMP
170–200°C / 340–390°F

WHOLE CROWN PRINCE SQUASH
Stuffed with Pumpkin Seeds & Chillies

My friend Gregg has been growing organic pumpkins and squash in Banbury, Oxfordshire, for years. He first introduced me to all the different varieties when I was cooking at The Lansdowne Pub in London's Primrose Hill many years ago. I went up for harvest one year and helped him load the fruit, packed in straw, into the hull of narrowboats he kept on the canal. They were the perfect fridges. These squash and pumpkins are now common on supermarket shelves and the world is a better place for it. I miss Gregg's early Sunday morning deliveries with squash, firewood and a few tequila shots.

1 large or 2 medium/small-sized Crown Prince squash (or use another squash such as Delicata, Kabocha or sweet Uchiki Kuri)

5 tbsp sunflower or olive oil

1 tsp ground cumin

1 tsp ground cinnamon

6 guajillo chillies, de-stemmed and deseeded

2 ancho chillies, de-stemmed and deseeded

2 pasilla chillies, de-stemmed and deseeded

250ml/1 cup hot water from the kettle

2 red onions, roughly chopped

4 garlic cloves, peeled

1 tsp dried Mexican oregano (or normal oregano)

3 tomatoes, chopped

100g/¾ cup pumpkin seeds

2 tbsp sesame seeds

Salt and freshly ground black pepper

To serve

Lime wedges

Sour cream

Cut a lid off the top of the squash and scrape out the seeds. Season the inside with salt and pepper, and rub with 1 tablespoon of the oil and ½ teaspoon each of the cumin and cinnamon. Loosely replace the squash lid, then place on the grill, close the lid and cook for 30 minutes until just about tender.

While the squash is cooking, toast all the chillies in the EGG for 5 minutes until fragrant, then remove and soak in the hot water for 10 minutes.

In a pan on the stove, cook the onions and garlic in 2 tablespoons of the oil for 5 minutes until softened, then add the oregano along with the remaining cumin and cinnamon, and cook for 1 minute until fragrant.

In a small food processor, blend the cooked onion mixture to a coarse purée with the tomatoes, half the pumpkin and sesame seeds, the soaked chillies (reserving the liquid), and salt and pepper to taste, adding a splash of the chilli soaking liquid if needed. Cook the purée in 1 tablespoon of the oil, in a small pan on the stove, for 5 minutes until thickened, then put to one side.

When the squash is almost cooked add the purée to the cavity, take the squash lid off and roast in the EGG for 15–30 minutes until completely tender.

While the squash is roasting, fry the remaining pumpkin seeds and sesame seeds in the remaining tablespoon of oil until they start to pop, then season to taste with salt and pepper and put to one side.

Serve the squash topped with the toasted seeds and with lime wedges and sour cream on the side.

PORK RIBS
with Ancho & Citrus Marinade

The only problem with this recipe is, no matter how many you make, you'll always want more. Also, don't try and keep yourself clean eating these. The mess is part of the fun.

SERVES 4–6

EGG SET UP
Indirect set-up; convEGGtor in legs-up position with the stainless-steel grill on top of the convEGGtor legs. You'll need a skillet.

TARGET TEMP
110–130°C / 230–265°F

1.5–2.5kg / 3lb 5oz–5½lb ribs, membrane removed, removed from fridge before lighting the EGG

For the dry rub
2 tsp ground cumin
2 tsp paprika
½ tsp ground black pepper

1 tsp ground allspice
2 tsp salt

For the ancho citrus marinade
2 dried ancho chillies, de-stemmed and deseeded
3 tomatoes, cut in half lengthways

1 small red onion, peeled and cut into 4 wedges
3 garlic cloves, unpeeled
½ tsp ground cinnamon
½ tsp ground cumin
2 tbsp vegetable or olive oil
Juice of ½ small orange
Juice of 1 small lime

Rub the ground spices and salt for the dry rub onto the ribs and put to one side.

Dry-fry the chillies in a moderately hot pan on the stove (or you can do this on the EGG's grill) for about 30 seconds until just browned and aromatic. Transfer to a bowl, cover with boiling water and set aside for about 10 minutes.

Grill, or dry-fry in a pan, the tomatoes, onion and garlic for 10 minutes until lightly charred. Peel the skin off the garlic and tomatoes, although it's fine to leave a few charred bits.

Drain the chillies and blend in a small food processor with the charred vegetables, the spices and about ½ teaspoon of salt, to make a smooth paste. Fry the paste in the oil for 10 minutes until thickened, then cool a bit and add the citrus juices. You want the marinade to have the texture of a thick sauce. Brush the ribs lightly with 3 tablespoons of the marinade.

Place on the grill, close the lid and cook for 1½–2 hours (when no rub smears off and the crust is stuck, then you're there). Transfer to a skillet, baste with some of the remaining citrus ancho marinade then add the rest to the skillet, cover in a double layer of foil and cook for about another 1–1½ hours until the internal temperature is 93–95°C / 200–203°F. Allow to rest for 30 minutes before serving with the cooking juices.

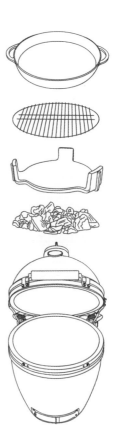

REVERSE SEAR STEAK PICANHA

SERVES 1

EGG SET UP
Indirect set-up; convEGGtor in legs-up position with the stainless-steel grill on top of the convEGGtor legs.

TARGET TEMP
110–130°C / 230–265°F, then 280–300°C / 535–570°F

Reverse sear is a cooking technique that allows you to better control the 'doneness' of your steak. The EGG is set at a low temperature to cook the picanha slowly until you reach the desired internal temperature. You then crank the EGG up to conventional steak-cooking heat and sear them off. This can work on any steak but make sure they are thick-cut, more than 5cm/2in thick. In the UK, picanha is often referred to as rump cap.

1 picanha steak (top sirloin cap), silver skin from the flesh side trimmed off (removed from fridge before lighting the EGG)

Salt and freshly ground black pepper

Season the steak generously with salt and pepper. Place straight on the grill, fat side up, close the lid and cook until the internal temperature reaches 48°C/118°F (for rare; see the chart below), about 35 minutes–1 hour.

Remove and rest in a warm place, wrapped in foil, while you increase the temperature of the EGG to 280°C/535°F. This is a good time to finish off any sides.

Return the steak fat side down to the grill, close the lid and colour for 2 minutes, then continue to cook for 2 minutes on each side until seared to your liking; probably just a few minutes. Rest for 15–20 minutes before slicing thinly to serve.

TEMPERATURE TEST FOR DONENESS
Cook the steak in the first stage to the following temperatures:

Rare: 48°C/118 °F
Medium-rare: 52°C/125°F
Medium: 58°C/136°F
Medium-well done: 63°C/145°F
Well done: 70°C/158°F

LAMB RIBS
with Tamarind Glaze

Another recipe where getting messy is part of the fun. The cooking times and method are very similar to the pork ribs from earlier in the chapter (page 131), so you might want to cook both at the same time. It's nice to serve them side by side.

2 racks of lamb ribs, about 800g/1¾lb each (you may think this is a lot but they shrink)

2 tbsp olive oil

2 garlic cloves, finely chopped

1 tsp toasted ground cumin seeds

2 tbsp toasted ground coriander seeds

Dried chilli flakes, to taste

1 tsp salt

Chilli sauce, to serve

For the tamarind glaze

150g/5¼oz tamarind paste (from a block, not a jar)

250ml/1 cup boiling water from the kettle

75g/6 tbsp brown sugar, plus extra to taste

1 tsp dried chilli flakes, plus extra to taste

1 garlic clove, very finely chopped

2 tbsp fish sauce (or use salt)

Salt, to taste

SERVES 4–6

EGG SET UP
Indirect set-up; convEGGtor in legs-up position with the stainless-steel grill on top of the convEGGtor legs, then remove the convEGGtor for direct set-up, to finish.

TARGET TEMP
110–130°C/230–265°F, then 220–250°C/430–480°F

Using a sharp knife, remove the membrane or flap from the bony side of the ribs.

Mix the oil, garlic, spices and salt, then rub this all over the ribs. Allow to marinate for at least 1 hour, but overnight, covered, in the fridge is best, bringing it back to room temperature before cooking.

Meanwhile, make the tamarind glaze. Break the tamarind into small pieces, place in a heatproof bowl and pour over the boiling water. Leave to soak for about 30 minutes, mashing it a bit every now with your fingers and removing any seeds or large fibres as you go. Strain, by pushing the tamarind through a sieve into a pan to remove (and discard) any remaining fibres and seeds. Add the sugar and remaining ingredients to the pulp, then gently cook until the sugar is dissolved, adding more sugar, salt or chilli to taste.

Place the lamb on the grill, close the lid and cook for 3 hours until soft, brushing with 50ml/3½ tbsp the tamarind glaze during the last hour.

Remove the lamb and rest for 10 minutes while you remove the convEGGtor, replace the grill for direct cooking, and increase the temperature to 220–250°C/430–480°F. Cut the lamb into ribs, brush with a little more glaze and then crisp on the grill with the lid closed for 2–5 minutes on each side, until sticky and beginning to char.

Serve with the remaining tamarind glaze, some chilli sauce, and a tangy green salad.

ROASTING

The indirect set-up here is the same as in the Low and Slow chapter, you are just cooking at a higher temperature. Again, the EGG shows why it's worth lighting simply because it cooks the food so well. I'm sure there is some detailed science behind how the EGG traps moisture in the food as well as it does, but I don't know what it is! All I can tell you is that there is something in the EGG's magic that keeps food from drying out.

Indirect set-up; convEGGtor in legs-up position with the stainless-steel grill on top of the convEGGtor legs. You'll need a skillet.

TARGET TEMP
120–140°C / 210–285°F

BUTTER-BATH CHICKEN
with Piri Piri

Not much to say about this other than it's chicken cooked in butter. What more do you need? It's absolutely delicious. Go to the effort of using the brine – it locks in the chicken's juiciness. Serve with cornbread (page 170) and hispi cabbage (page 106).

10 bone-in, skin-on chicken thighs

1 quantity brine (page 62) or 50g / ⅛ cup salt dissolved in 500ml / 2 cups water

1 tsp chilli powder, or more or less to taste

1 tbsp paprika

1 tsp ground cumin

250g / generous 1 cup butter, melted

6 garlic cloves, peeled and squashed

2 bay leaves

1 tbsp honey

2 tbsp piri piri sauce (or use BBQ sauce)

Submerge the chicken in the brine and leave for 1–4 hours, then remove and pat dry.

Rub the spices all over the chicken, then put in a skillet with the melted butter, garlic and bay leaves, making sure the ingredients come no more than halfway up the pan. Put on the grill, close the lid and cook for 1 hour.

Remove the chicken from the butter and coat it in the honey and piri piri sauce, then cook on the grill for 20–45 minutes until deeply coloured, turning a few times; the internal temperature should be 75°C / 167°F. Place back in the skillet and rest for 10 minutes before serving.

ROASTED PARTRIDGE
with 'Nduja, Sultanas & Sweet Marsala

SERVES 4

EGG SET UP
Indirect set-up; convEGGtor in legs-
up position with the stainless-steel
grill on top of the convEGGtor legs.

TARGET TEMP
200°C / 390°F

This is a great way to hone your grilling skills on a whole bird.
When you are checking the temperature, get the probe into the
thickest part of the leg. The most likely error in this recipe is that
you overcook the birds. Err on the side of caution and allow for a
long rest.

40g / 1½oz sultanas
(golden raisins)
or raisins

4 partridge

40g / 1½oz 'Nduja
(or spiced chorizo)

40ml / 2½ tbsp sweet
Marsala or sherry

20g / ¼ cup flaked
(slivered) almonds

2 garlic cloves, finely
chopped

4 rashers (slices) of
streaky bacon

Salt and freshly ground
black pepper

Cover the sultanas or raisins with hot water from the kettle and
leave to soak for 10 minutes, then drain.

Season the partridge with salt and pepper inside and out. Mix the
'Nduja with the drained sultanas, Marsala or sherry, almonds and
garlic, and add salt and pepper to taste. Stuff the birds with the
'Nduja mixture.

Stretch the bacon using the back of a knife to press it longer and
wider, then wrap the bacon around the partridge, making sure the
breasts are covered.

Place the partridge on the grill on their backs, close the lid and
cook for about 15 minutes, then remove the bacon (reserve to
serve with the bird) and switch to cooking breast side down for
about 10–15 minutes until a thermometer registers an internal
temperature of 74°C / 165°F and the juices run clear. Rest for
15 minutes in a warm place before serving with the bacon.

DOUBLE-COOK LAMB KEBAB
with Chopped Salad & Paratha

This is a variation on 'cag', a type of Turkish kebab similar to a doner but cooked horizontally, like a shawarma. The thing that makes it different is that the meat is threaded onto a skewer while being cut, then served on the skewer. There will come a point where you can't carve any more meat directly on to the skewer. Shred the rest and serve it separately.

1 bone-in shoulder of lamb, about 2.5kg/5½lb (although mutton or ex-dairy goat would more authentic)

1 onion, very finely chopped

150g/⅔ cup plain yogurt

2 green (bell) peppers, halved

Salt and freshly ground black pepper

Oil, for grilling

To serve

2 onions, thinly sliced

1 lemon

2–3 tomatoes, sliced

Parathas (page 173)

Chilli sauce

Rub the lamb with salt and pepper, the onion and the yogurt, then cover and allow to marinate in the fridge for at least 4 hours, but ideally overnight or up to 12 hours, removing it to come to room temperature before cooking.

Oil the grill lightly and place the lamb on it. Close the lid and cook for 3–4 hours until the internal temperature is about 90°C/194°F, or until tender but not spoon-soft; you want it to have a bit of texture. After about 1½ hours, check that it is not colouring too deeply, wrapping in foil if that is the case.

While the meat is cooking, rub a big pinch of salt into the sliced onions and allow to sit for a couple of minutes, then rinse in cold water, drain and then squeeze over the juice of half the lemon.

Remove the meat from the grill and allow to rest for about 1 hour. Increase the heat to around 200°C/390°F and pop the green peppers in for about 20–30 minutes to roast. You can also cook the parathas at this point.

15 minutes before the lamb resting time is up, remove the convEGGtor and put the grill in place. At this point peel the green peppers, remove the seeds and cut into thick strips.

Insert long metal skewers lengthways into the meat and carve off strips about 2cm/¾in thick, placing them on a tray. Check the seasoning, adding salt and paper to taste.

Add the meat to the grill, close the lid and cook for about 2 minutes on each side until nicely browned, then serve on top of parathas with slices of tomato and onion and the green pepper strips, with the remaining lemon half cut into wedges, and chilli sauce on the side.

SERVES 6–8

EGG SET UP
Indirect set-up; convEGGtor in legs-up position with the stainless-steel grill on top of the convEGGtor legs; then remove the convEGGtor for direct set-up.

TARGET TEMP
130–150°C/265–300°F, then 200°C/390°F

FISH EN PAPILLOTE
with Provence Flavours

Yes, it's a bit of a faff putting these together, but it is worth it.
All the flavour is locked in the bag and it feels like opening a gift.

16 prawns (shrimp), peeled and deveined (heads and shells reserved)

100g / scant ½ cup butter, at room temperature

800g / 1¾lb fish fillet, in 4 portions, skin on if small fish

1 fennel bulb, trimmed and thinly sliced (or use leek)

2 garlic cloves, very thinly sliced

12 cherry tomatoes, finely chopped

4 bay leaves

4 small sprigs of thyme

1 small red chilli, deseeded and finely chopped

4 pared strips of orange zest

50g / 1¾oz marsh samphire or spinach leaves (optional)

Salt and freshly ground black pepper

Put the prawn heads and shells in a skillet, add to the grill, close the lid and roast for about 20 minutes until crisp and aromatic. Add the butter and stir well, cook for 1 minute and remove from the grill to infuse in a warm place for 30 minutes, then strain the butter into a bowl, discarding the shells.

Prepare the parcels all at once, or one at a time, depending on how much work surface you have. Place 4 large sheets of foil or baking parchment (A3 / ledger size) lengthways on the work surface and place a fish portion in each.

Divide the fennel, garlic, tomatoes, bay, thyme, chilli and orange zest between the parcels, add 4 prawns to each, sprinkle over the samphire or spinach, if using, and spoon over the infused butter. Add salt and pepper to taste, fold the foil over double and fold all sides inwards twice, to create an airtight package. (You can store the packages in the fridge at this point, until needed.)

Carefully place the packages on the grill, close the lid and cook for 12–15 minutes; the packages will have puffed up.

Place the packages straight onto individual plates to cut open at the table, taking care of the hot steam and juices. Serve with toasted baguette or boiled potatoes.

EGG SET UP
Indirect set-up; convEGGtor in legs-up position with the stainless-steel grill on top of the convEGGtor legs.

TARGET TEMP
140–170°C / 285–340°F

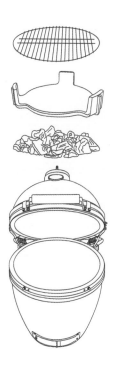

ROAST LEG OF HOGGET
Crying over Hasselback Potatoes

SERVES 8–10

EGG SET UP
Indirect set-up; convEGGtor in legs-up position with the stainless-steel grill on top of the convEGGtor legs.

TARGET TEMP
180–210°C / 355–410°F,
then 250–300°C / 480–570°F
(optional)

Hoggets are sheep over a year old and younger than two, and I would take hogget over lamb any day. As the animals get older, they lose that inherent fattiness of lamb and, with the extra year of life, are allowed to develop a more nuanced flavour.

If you want to make a gravy to go with this dish, remove the potatoes from the roasting pan once they are crisp and pour in 300ml/1¼ cups stock. Scrape the bottom of the roasting pan with a wooden spoon while the stock reduces and, once it's reduced by half, pour in any resting juices from the hogget and serve.

1 leg of hogget, about 2.5–3kg / 5½lb–6lb 10oz

3–4 garlic cloves, sliced

50g / 3½ tbsp softened butter, or olive oil

1kg / 2lb 2oz waxy potatoes

300g / 10½oz baby onions or little shallots, peeled and left whole (optional, but nice)

Big bunch of rosemary sprigs

400ml / 1⅔ cups chicken or hogget stock, white wine or water

Salt and freshly ground black pepper

Rub salt and pepper all over the hogget. Using a pointed knife, stab small, deep slits about 5cm/2in apart all over the leg, inserting a slice of garlic deep into each slit, then smear with the softened butter or olive oil.

Place the meat on a rack set over a roasting pan to catch the meat juices. Place in the EGG, close the lid and cook for about 20–30 minutes while you prepare the potatoes and onions, if using.

Make slices into each potato about 5mm/⅛in apart, making sure you cut only three-quarters of the way through so the potatoes stay connected at the bottom and fan out a bit as they cook. Put them in a bowl with the onions, if using, toss together and season with salt and pepper, adding any leftover garlic.

Remove the roasting pan from the EGG, add the rosemary sprigs, potatoes and onions to the pan and pour over the stock. Put the roasting pan back underneath the leg so that the meat is 'crying' over the vegetables and roast for about another 1–1½ hours, depending on how well you like your meat cooked.

Remove the meat and allow it to rest, then crank the temperature up to about 250–300°C / 480–570°F, to crisp the potatoes a bit if needed (and you can colour the leg for 5 minutes too if you like).

EGG SET UP
Indirect set-up; convEGGtor in legs-up position with the stainless-steel grill on top of the convEGGtor legs.

TARGET TEMP
180–210°C / 355–410°F

FILLED BAKED POTATOES:
Tartiflette or Roasted Shallot, Bone Marrow & Rosemary

These are great on their own or make a superb side for a dirty steak or piece of smoked pork.

4 medium baking potatoes (or another fluffy variety)

Salt and freshly ground black pepper

Filling 1: Tartiflette

2 tbsp butter

100ml / generous ⅓ cup thick double (heavy) cream

4 slices smoked cured or cooked ham, roughly chopped

200g / 7oz soft or semi-soft mountain cheese such as reblochon, raclette or taleggio, grated or torn depending on type

Small bunch of flat-leaf parsley, roughly chopped

Filling 2: Roasted Shallot, Bone Marrow & Rosemary

3 large banana shallots, unpeeled

1 sprig of rosemary, leaves finely chopped

1 garlic clove, finely chopped

8 pieces of bone marrow (about 3cm / 1¼in long) removed from the bone, or use lardo or fatty bacon

Place the potatoes on the grill, close the lid and bake for about 40 minutes–1 hour, until cooked and the skins are crispy.

For the Tartiflette filling, cut the potatoes in half and use a spoon to scoop out the flesh, leaving the skin unbroken. Roughly mash the flesh and gently mix in the butter, cream, ham and cheese, and season with pepper and a little salt.

Carefully spoon the mixture back into the potato skins. Cook in the EGG for 10–15 minutes until golden and bubbling at the top. Serve immediately, sprinkled with the parsley, perhaps with a little Dijon mustard and cornichons on the table.

For the Roasted Shallot filling, bake the shallots alongside the potatoes in the EGG as above, for about 30 minutes until completely soft, then set aside until cool enough to handle. Peel and roughly chop, season with salt and pepper, add the chopped rosemary and garlic and leave to one side.

Scoop out the potato flesh as described above, into a bowl. Gently mix in the bone marrow and the roasted shallot mixture then carefully spoon the mixture back into the potato skins. Cook in the EGG for 10–15 minutes until golden and bubbling at the top. Serve immediately (I like to serve these alongside steak).

WHOLE CARROTS
with Zhug

Here the EGG's ability to do amazing things with vegetables is on show again. This would make a great side for the hogget dish on page 144, or as part of a mezze. This recipe will also work with parsnips and little beetroot.

12 medium carrots (good quality from a bunch; multi-coloured can be nice)

2 tbsp sunflower or olive oil

Leaves from a few sprigs of thyme

1 tbsp butter

1 tbsp honey

Big pinch of dried chilli flakes (Aleppo or Urfa are nice)

Grated zest of 1 lemon or orange

½ small bunch of herbs, such tarragon, chives or flat-leaf parsley, roughly chopped (optional)

Salt and freshly ground black pepper

Zhug (page 190), or you could use chimichurri (page 190) or dukka (page 187), to serve

Put the carrots in a large bowl. Toss with the oil, thyme and salt and pepper to taste. Spread over a roasting pan so they sit in a single layer, add to the grill, close the lid and roast for 30 minutes, turning halfway, until tender.

Toss in the butter, honey, chilli flakes and lemon or orange zest and return to the EGG for 5 more minutes until browned.

Stir through the herbs, if using, just before serving, and serve on a plate or platter, drizzled with the zhug (or chimichurri or dukka).

SERVES 6 AS A SIDE
or as part of a mezze

EGG SET UP
Indirect set-up; convEGGtor in legs-up position with the stainless-steel grill on top of the convEGGtor legs.

TARGET TEMP
150–180°C / 300–355°F

CORN
with Kikos Crumbs

**SERVES 4–8 AS A
STARTER OR SIDE**

EGG SET UP
Indirect set-up; convEGGtor in legs-up position with the stainless-steel grill on top of the convEGGtor legs, then remove the convEGGtor for a direct set-up, to char the corn on the grill

TARGET TEMP
160–210°C / 320–410°F

This is a great dish that requires very little work. The corn cobs are prefect on their own but I prefer them as a side dish or as part of a larger spread. The kikos (fried salted maize snacks) are optional, but are a great savoury hit crushed and sprinkled over loads of dishes, and of course as a snack; you can find them in plenty of shops.

8 ears of corn, unhusked

1 tbsp chipotle in adobo, or use dried chipotle chilli flakes or paste, plus extra (optional) to serve

100g / scant ½ cup mayonnaise, or roasted garlic alioli (page 183)

Vegetable oil, for brushing

100g / 3½oz strong, salty cheese, such as feta, Parmesan, Cheddar, coarsely grated or crumbled

Small bunch of coriander (cilantro), finely chopped

4 tbsp kikos, crushed to a powder

Salt and freshly ground black pepper

2 limes, cut into wedges, to serve

Place the corn cobs inside their husks on the grill, close the lid and cook for 20–25 minutes until tender. Allow to cool for 5 minutes, then pull the husks down, leaving them attached to the base of the cob, removing all of the silk. Carefully remove the convEGGtor and replace the grill.

While the corn is cooking, mix the chipotle (crush it if whole) into the mayonnaise.

Brush the corn with oil, season with salt and pepper to taste and place on the grill. Close the lid and cook, turning occasionally with tongs, until lightly charred, for about 10 minutes.

Remove from the grill and either skewer or insert corn forks, then immediately coat each corn with the mayonnaise. Sprinkle each with cheese, coriander and extra chilli, if you like, and with the crushed kikos. Serve with lime wedges on the side.

LEFTOVERS MOUSSAKA

There is no excuse for throwing meat away. Especially when leftovers can be this delicious.

Smoky aubergines, smoky leftover meat, smoky yogurt topping. Oh boy. I can eat an awful lot of moussaka in a single sitting.

2 small onions, sliced

2 big garlic cloves, finely sliced

4–6 tbsp olive oil

400g/14oz tomato passata (purée)

2 tsp dried oregano

1½ tsp ground cinnamon

About 500g/1lb 2oz leftover roast lamb, mutton or goat (or beef), finely chopped

2 large aubergines (eggplant), sliced 1cm/⅜in thick and lightly salted

Small bunch of flat-leaf parsley, roughly chopped

Salt and freshly ground black pepper

For the topping

500g/generous 2 cups Greek yogurt

2 medium eggs, beaten

1 tbsp cornflour (cornstarch)

100g/3½oz halloumi, coarsely grated

¼ nutmeg, finely grated

Fry the onions and garlic in 2 tablespoons of the oil in a pan on the stove for 10 minutes until soft. Add the tomato passata, half the oregano and the cinnamon and cook for 2 minutes, then stir well, season to taste with salt and pepper and remove from the heat. Stir through the chopped meat and leave to one side.

Whisk the yogurt for the topping with the eggs and cornflour in a medium bowl, then stir in the grated halloumi along with the grated nutmeg and plenty of freshly ground black pepper.

Brush the aubergine slices with olive oil, place on the grill, close the lid and cook for 4–6 minutes on each side until soft and golden brown.

Arrange a third of the aubergines in the base of a dish and top with half of the meat and tomato sauce. Repeat these layers, finishing off with a final layer of aubergine. Spread the yogurt mixture over the top, scatter with the remaining dried oregano and spoon over a final tablespoon of olive oil.

Place on the grill, close the lid and bake for 25–35 minutes until the top is golden and blistered. Remove and rest for 10 minutes or so before scattering with parsley and serving.

SERVES 6–8

EGG SET UP
Make the sauce and topping before lighting the EGG and grilling the aubergine.

Indirect set-up; convEGGtor in legs-up position with the stainless-steel grill on top of the convEGGtor legs.

TARGET TEMP
150–180°C/300–355°F

BAKED WHOLE BEETROOT

Do not skip past this recipe just because it's focused on the humble beetroot. The EGG excels at cooking vegetables. Serve with tahini sauce (page 183), horseradish crème fraîche, or smoked ricotta (page 99).

2 bunches of beetroot (beet), leaves and stems cut off and reserved

2 garlic cloves, finely chopped

1 tbsp finely chopped fresh thyme

2 tbsp Dijon mustard

3 tbsp red wine vinegar (or balsamic)

30ml/2 tbsp olive oil, plus extra to serve

Salt and freshly ground black pepper

Place the beetroot on the grill, close the lid and bake for around 45 minutes–1½ hours until tender.

Meanwhile, trim the beetroot tops, removing any discoloured stalk or leaves, and give them a good wash to remove any grit.

Bring a big pan of salted water to the boil on the stove and boil the stems and leaves in their entirety for 30 seconds, then drain and set aside.

Once the beetroot are cooked and cool enough to handle, peel them. Make slices in each beetroot about 5mm/⅛in apart, making sure you cut only three-quarters of the way through so they stay connected at the bottom and fan out a bit as they cook. Dress them with the garlic, thyme, mustard, vinegar, olive oil and salt and pepper to taste, then return to the EGG in a small metal pan. Close the lid and cook for 2–3 minutes until crisp, turning once.

Serve the baked beetroot alongside the whole stems.

EGG SET UP
Indirect set-up; convEGGtor in legs-up position with the stainless-steel grill on top of the convEGGtor legs.

TARGET TEMP
200–220°C / 390–430°F

DUTCH OVEN

Dutch oven refers to the cooking pot itself, rather than any cooking appliance. They are traditionally made of heavy-duty materials, like cast iron, and referred to in English as casserole dishes – confusingly, as casserole is the French word for 'pan'.

On the face of it, cooking in a pot inside an EGG may seem unnecessary. After all, won't a conventional oven just do the same job? There are two main reasons why the answer is no. Firstly, instead of browning the meat in the pot, you can use the grill, which helps add some lovely caramelization to the ingredients, and secondly, you get that extra layer of flavour the smoke adds to the cook, giving the dish much more depth. In general, the Dutch oven cooks without its own lid. You can also double up here and use the grill to cook the side dishes.

SERVES 6–8

EGG SET UP
Indirect set-up; convEGGtor in legs-up position with the stainless-steel grill on top of the convEGGtor legs. You'll need a Dutch oven.

TARGET TEMP
200–210°C / 390–410°F, then 130C–150°C / 265–300°F

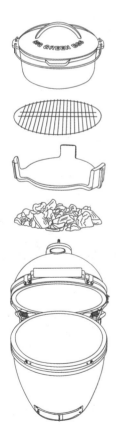

FEATHERBLADE CARBONNADE À LA FLAMANDE

You'll see that this recipe calls for a drop in temperature during the cook, which is achievable because of the length of time the meat is cooking for. Close the top and bottom vents to a minimum until the EGG gets down to 130–150°C / 265–300°F. Sweet, sharp and boozy, this recipe is a delight. Serve with pasta, noodles, potatoes or dumplings, with more mustard at the table.

2 tbsp flour (wholemeal can be nice) plus another 1 tbsp if you want a thicker sauce

3 onions, thinly sliced

Piece of featherblade steak, about 1.5–2kg / 3lb 5oz–4lb 6oz (or use a boneless piece of beef shin or chuck), removed from fridge before lighting the EGG

3 garlic cloves, thinly sliced

2 tbsp vegetable oil or beef dripping

2 bay leaves

1 sprig of thyme

30g / 2½ tbsp brown sugar

1 tbsp cider vinegar or wine vinegar

1 tbsp Dijon mustard, plus extra to taste and serve

200ml / generous ¾ cup chicken, veal or beef stock

660ml / 2½ cups dark Belgian-style beer, or your favourite ale

Salt and freshly ground black pepper

Place the Dutch oven in the EGG to preheat for 10 minutes. Meanwhile, season the flour with salt and pepper and toss the sliced onions in it. Place the meat on a large plate.

Add the steak to the grill, close the EGG lid and brown for 5–6 minutes on each side. Remove the steak back to the plate. At the same time, brown the onions and garlic in the oil or dripping in the pot, with the bay leaves and thyme added, for 10–15 minutes until soft, opening every few minutes to give a stir. Add the sugar and vinegar and cook for a further 3–5 minutes until the liquid has nearly evaporated, then stir through the mustard and the additional tablespoon of flour, if using.

Return the meat (along with any juices on the plate) to the pot, add the stock and beer and season to taste, then close the EGG's lid. Adjust the vents for a target temperature of 130C–150°C / 265–300°F.

Cook for 3–4 hours until the meat is very tender but not falling apart (the internal temperature should read about 93°C / 200°F). Check a couple of times during cooking to make sure it has plenty of sauce and is not drying out – if needed, add a little water (or more stock) to ensure the meat is at least half covered at all times. Allow to rest for 10 minutes, then add salt, pepper and more mustard to taste. Serve in slices with the sauce.

ROAST ROOT SOUP
with Pepper Butter

A perfect way to use up a mish-mash of veg from the fridge. Throwing them on the grill breathes new life into slightly sad-looking vegetables. Play around with the individual quantities, and add beetroot (beet), radishes, swede (rutabaga), fennel, kohlrabi, Jerusalem artichokes and even fresh ginger or turmeric.

1 leek, trimmed and rinsed

1 head of garlic

2 small onions, unpeeled

16 baby (or 8 small) carrots (a mix of colours is nice), scrubbed and halved lengthways

1 small celeriac (celery root), peeled and sliced 1cm/⅜in thick

2 parsnips, peeled and sliced 1cm/⅜in thick

1 small squash, peeled, deseeded and sliced 1cm/⅜in thick

2 tbsp olive oil

1.5l/6½ cups hot chicken or vegetable stock

2 bay leaves

Big sprig of thyme, sage or rosemary

Salt and freshly ground black pepper

Crusty bread, to serve

For the pepper butter

100g/scant ½ cup unsalted butter, at room temperature

1 tsp flaky salt

1 tsp coarsely ground black pepper

SERVES 6–8

EGG SET UP
Indirect set-up; convEGGtor in legs-up position with the stainless-steel grill on top of the convEGGtor legs. You'll need a Dutch oven.

TARGET TEMP
160–190°C / 320–375°F

Place the leek, garlic and onions on the back of the grill, close the lid and cook for 20 minutes until soft, turning occasionally.

Meanwhile, brush or toss the carrots and sliced vegetables with the olive oil and season with salt and pepper. Grill for about 6 minutes on each side, while the other vegetables are roasting.

While the veg are grilling, make the pepper butter. Beat the butter until smooth and creamy, then mix in the salt and pepper and roll into a log in baking parchment.

When the grilled vegetables are ready, place them in a Dutch oven, reserving a few carrot halves and slices of each vegetable, to finish the soup. Remove the skin of the roasted leek, onions and garlic (squeezing out the soft flesh after snipping off the papery tops is easiest), roughly chop and add to the grilled vegetables in the pot along with half the pepper butter.

Place the pot on the grill and add the hot stock, bay leaves and sprig of herbs. Close the EGG's lid and cook for 15 minutes. Remove from the EGG and remove the bay and herbs. Blend to a smooth purée, adding more water or stock if needed, then return the soup to the EGG to warm through if necessary.

Spoon into bowls and top with the reserved vegetables. Serve with crusty bread and the remaining pepper butter.

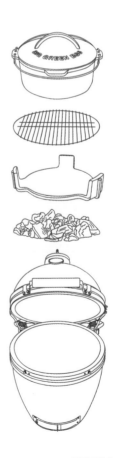

EGG SET UP
Indirect set-up; convEGGtor in legs-up position with the stainless-steel grill on top of the convEGGtor legs. You'll need a Dutch oven.

TARGET TEMP
140–170°C / 285–340°F

COCONUT & HABANERO BLACK BEANS

This has its roots in a Jamaican black bean curry. You want it to be quite wet. Serve with rice and the paratha on page 173.

3 tbsp coconut or sunflower oil

1 onion, finely chopped

1 green (bell) pepper, finely chopped

3 garlic cloves, finely chopped

1 habanero or Scotch bonnet chilli (or use another chilli for less heat), finely chopped

2 tsp ground cumin

2 bay leaves

250g / 1½ cups dried black (turtle) beans, soaked in plenty of cold water overnight

200ml / generous ¾ cup coconut milk

Juice of ½ lime, plus extra to taste

100g / 3½oz fresh spinach, chopped

Small bunch of coriander (cilantro), roughly chopped

Salt and freshly ground black pepper

Heat the oil in a Dutch oven on the stove, add the onion, green pepper, garlic and chilli and cook for 10 minutes until soft, then add the cumin and bay leaves.

Drain the soaked beans, rinse and add to the pot with enough fresh cold water to cover the beans by at least 5cm/2in. Bring to a boil on the stove, skimming off any froth that appears, then place a lid on and transfer to the EGG for 1½–2 hours, or until the beans are tender. If the beans get too dry, top up with more water.

Once the beans are cooked, add salt and pepper to taste, stir in the coconut milk and lime juice, then cook in the EGG for a further 10 minutes.

Stir in the spinach and half the coriander, and cook just until wilted, about 2 minutes. Remove, season with salt and pepper to taste, scatter over the remaining coriander and add a final squeeze of lime juice.

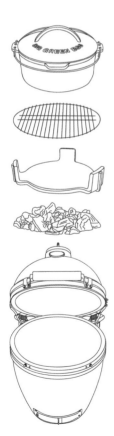

TRINI DUCK CURRY

SERVES 6–8

EGG SET UP
Direct set-up with the stainless-steel grill in place. You'll need a Dutch oven.

TARGET TEMP
180–200°C / 355–390°F

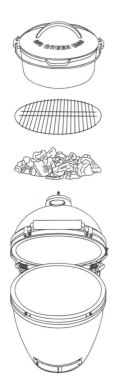

I've been lucky enough to visit Trinidad a few times, working to promote their goat meat industry. Trini food culture is fascinating and undervalued in the world, and I am grateful to Franka, Ardene and the team for introducing me to it. I was visiting a farm one afternoon when I was called round the back of the office. In the courtyard, Ravi, the farm manager, and a few friends were cooking lunch. With the aid of an enormous cleaver, an open fire that was half tandoor, half Kamado, and a wok, he cooked up a delicious duck curry in about an hour. It is the only thing that I've ever seen happen quickly in Trinidad.

The trick here is to boil it hard. I know, it doesn't sound right, but it is. Trini food can be fiery, and this is meant to be hot, but the fresh green chillies give a zesty heat, not a face-melting one. Don't skimp on them. Serve with the paratha on page 173.

4 duck legs, about 1.2kg / 2½lb in total, chopped into bite-sized pieces on the bone (use a good cleaver, or ask your butcher to do this)

Juice of 1 lime, plus extra to serve

3 garlic cloves, finely chopped

1 tsp salt

1 tsp freshly ground black pepper

2 tbsp Trinidad curry powder (or use another curry powder)

1 tbsp amchur (mango) powder or chaat masala (or add another squeeze of lime juice and 1 tsp garam masala)

2 tsp ground turmeric

1–2 tsp hot sauce

½ bunch of spring onions (scallions), finely chopped

2 green chillies, finely chopped (use Scotch bonnet for extra flavour and lots of extra heat)

Small bunch of coriander (cilantro), stalks and leaves separated and finely chopped

1 tsp fresh thyme leaves, finely chopped

2 tbsp vegetable or coconut oil

1 x 400ml / 14oz can of coconut milk

In a bowl or dish, mix the duck with the lime juice, garlic, salt, pepper, spices and hot sauce. Stir through the spring onions, chillies, chopped coriander stalks and thyme, then cover and marinate for at least 2 hours, or overnight in the fridge.

Heat a Dutch oven in the EGG for 5 minutes, then add the oil and stir in the duck and its marinade. Close the EGG's lid, cook for 5 minutes, then stir and cook for 10–15 minutes until beginning to colour and fry. Add enough water to cover the meat, close the EGG's lid and cook for 30 minutes until rich and thick. Pour in the coconut milk, close the EGG's lid and cook for another 30 minutes –1 hour until the duck is tender, adding a splash more water if it dries out.

Serve topped with the chopped coriander leaves and extra lime juice squeezed over.

LAMB CHOP BHUNA

This recipe isn't mine, it's my friend Shanti Bhushan's. Shanti is the Executive Chef of Brigadiers, the best curry house in London. Although to call it a curry house is slightly underselling it. It's a magnificent place. We cooked a goat version of this dish together at Meatopia, the London BBQ festival, and it's one of the finest things I have ever eaten. I have learned so much from Shanti about Indian food.

Grilling the chops before they go in the pot is essential to lock in that smoky flavour.

EGG SET UP
Indirect set-up; convEGGtor in legs-up position with the stainless-steel grill on top of the convEGGtor legs. You'll need a Dutch oven.

TARGET TEMP
190–210°C / 375–410°F

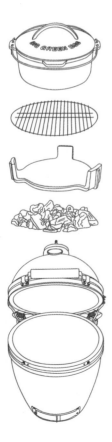

50g / 3½ tbsp ghee	2 tbsp garam masala	**To serve**
3 green cardamom pods	2 bay leaves	Paratha (page 173)
½ cinnamon stick	500ml / 2 cups water	Mint raita (page 187)
½ blade of mace	1kg / 2lb 2oz lamb chops	Harissa (page 186), or Charred salsa (page 188)
1 large onion, finely chopped	200g / scant 1 cup plain yogurt	Salad of your choice
5 garlic cloves, finely chopped	4 whole mild dried red chillies (such as Kashmiri)	
1 tbsp finely grated fresh ginger	1 green chilli, finely chopped	
2 tsp Kashmiri chilli powder	Salt	

Heat a Dutch oven in the EGG for at least 15 minutes, then add the ghee, stir in all the whole spices and cook for 30 seconds until fragrant. Add the onion, close the EGG's lid and cook for 10–20 minutes, stirring a couple of times until soft and lightly golden.

Add the garlic, ginger, 1 teaspoon of salt, the chilli powder, garam masala and bay leaves with 100ml / ⅓ cup of the water and cook, stirring a few times until the oil comes to the surface.

Season the chops with salt and cook directly on the grill until lightly coloured. Add the yogurt to the pot and stir until evaporated and creamy. Add the dried red chillies, the chops and the remaining water to the pot, close the EGG's lid and cook for 1–1½ hours until the chops are tender.

Stir through the chopped green chilli and season to taste with salt, then serve with paratha, mint raita, harissa or charred salsa and salad.

MOLE

EGG SET UP
Indirect set-up; convEGGtor in legs-up position with the stainless-steel grill on top of the convEGGtor legs. You'll need a Dutch oven.

TARGET TEMP
180–200°C / 355–390°F

Cooking this in the EGG, especially the charring of the garlic and tomatoes, adds smokiness to the finished dish, which really complements the spice mix. Serve with the soft tortillas on page 179 and the corn on page 148.

2 ancho chillies

2 pasilla chillies

3 tomatoes

1 red onion, base sliced off

1 head of garlic

3 tbsp oil

1 tsp annatto seeds

50g / ⅓ cup raisins

100ml / generous ⅓ cup water

1 tsp ground cinnamon

1 tsp dried Mexican oregano

1 tsp toasted dried guajillo chilli flakes

1 tsp toasted pasilla chilli powder

½ tsp ground allspice

¼ tsp ground cloves

½ tsp ground thyme

¼ tsp ground bay

½ tsp ground toasted cumin seeds

1 tbsp sesame seeds

½ tsp salt

250ml / 1 cup chicken stock (or water)

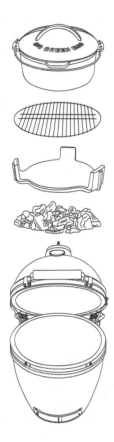

Toast all the whole chillies on the grill for 1 minute. Remove the stems and seeds, place in a bowl and cover in freshly boiled water from the kettle. Leave to soak. Char the tomatoes, onion and garlic bulb on the grill for 10 minutes or until the skin is charred and the flesh is soft.

Heat the oil in a small pan and fry the annatto seeds for 30 seconds or until the oil is a deep red colour. Strain the oil into a bowl (discarding the seeds) then leave to one side.

Snip the papery tops off the garlic and squeeze out the flesh. Peel the onion and tomatoes and, in a food processor or blender, blend the charred vegetables with the soaked chillies (discarding the soaking liquid), raisins, water, spices and herbs, sesame seeds and salt, to make a smooth sauce.

Add the strained oil to a Dutch oven on the grill and cook the blended sauce for 5 minutes or until most of the liquid has evaporated and the sauce is beginning to brown and stick to the bottom of the pot. Stir the stock or water into the mole and cook for 10 minutes or until the sauce is rich and thick.

FISH CURRY

I use frozen fish fillets for this. It's a great way to use fish that might need a little help to get the best out of it.

For the spice blend

2 tsp uncooked basmati rice

1 tsp dried chilli flakes

2 tsp coriander seeds

2 tsp cumin seeds

1 tsp black peppercorns

1 tsp black mustard seeds

1 tsp fennel seeds

2 cloves

1 tsp ground turmeric

For the curry

650g/1lb 7oz fish fillets (defrosted if frozen)

1½ tsp salt

3 tomatoes

1 onion, base sliced off

2 red chillies

2 garlic cloves, roughly chopped

1 tbsp grated fresh ginger

2 tbsp coconut or vegetable oil

10 curry leaves (optional)

200ml/generous ¾ cup full-fat coconut milk

Juice of 1 lime

SERVES 4–6

EGG SET UP
Indirect set-up; convEGGtor in legs-up position with the stainless-steel grill on top of the convEGGtor legs. You'll need a Dutch oven.

TARGET TEMP
180–200°C/355–390°F

Toast the rice and spices in a skillet in the EGG for 2–3 minutes until they become aromatic, then grind to a powder using a pestle and mortar or a spice grinder.

Coat the fish fillets in 2 tablespoons of the spice blend and ½ teaspoon of the salt, and leave to one side. Put the whole tomatoes, onion and chillies on the grill, close the lid and roast for 5 minutes until charred and softened. In a food processor or blender, blend the charred vegetables with the remaining teaspoon of salt, the garlic, ginger and the remaining spice blend to a smooth paste (adding a splash of water if necessary).

Heat the oil in a Dutch oven, add the curry leaves, if using, and cook for 1 minute until they sizzle, then add the spice paste, close the EGG's lid and cook for 10–15 minutes, until it begins to stick to the pot. Add the coconut milk and simmer for 20 minutes until the sauce starts to thicken.

Either poach the fish in the sauce for 3–4 minutes until just cooked, or cook on the grill with the lid closed for 3 minutes, then add to the sauce. Add lime juice to taste.

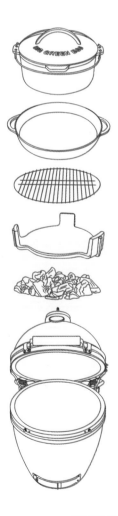

A handmade 'kama' – the iron pot that sits in the hole in the top of a traditional Kamado oven, and which is commonly used to make the Japanese rice dish kamameshi (page 166).

KAMAMESHI

SERVES 4

EGG SET UP
Indirect set-up; convEGGtor in legs-up position with the stainless-steel grill on top of the convEGGtor legs. You'll need a Dutch oven.

TARGET TEMP
160–180°C / 320–355°F

Kamameshi is a dish that had to make it into the book. It is cooked in a 'kama', the iron pot that sits in the hole in the top of a traditional Kamado (see photos on pages 164–165). It's somewhere between a pilaf and risotto and should be quite wet. A wholesome, warming, filling dish. Serve it direct from the grill to the table.

250g / 1½ cups Japanese short-grain rice

4 boneless chicken thighs, each cut into 2

2 tbsp light soy sauce

2 tbsp mirin

2 tbsp sake

1 tsp salt

500ml / 2 cups chicken stock

Bunch of spring onions (scallions), cut into 3cm / 1¼in lengths

1 garlic clove, finely chopped

2 carrots, thinly sliced

100g / 3½oz peas or beans

50g / 1¾oz shiitake mushrooms, sliced

Wash the rice and leave to drain for 30 minutes.

Put the chicken in a Dutch oven, add the soy sauce, mirin, sake and salt and mix into the chicken. Place on the grill, close the EGG's lid and allow to get hot through. Once hot, tip in the rice and the remaining ingredients. Close the lid and cook for 20–25 minutes, or until all the liquid is absorbed.

Leave the pot in the EGG, lid closed, for 5–10 minutes, for the rice to crust, then remove and allow to rest for 5 minutes before serving.

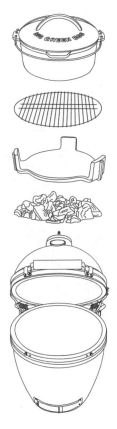

MUTTON SHOULDER
with Melting Onions, Rosemary & Honey

You could substitute lamb here, but mutton is easy to get hold of from online suppliers if your butcher doesn't stock it, and has a richness in flavour and texture with which lamb simply cannot compete.

1 shoulder of mutton, about 1.5–2kg/ 3lb 5oz–4lb 6oz

4 sprigs of rosemary

3 garlic cloves, peeled and quartered

800g/1¾lb red onions, peeled and quartered with root ends left attached

250ml/1 cup white wine

6 tbsp honey

Salt and freshly ground black pepper

Use a small knife to stab the mutton all over. Stuff the slits with half the rosemary leaves and the garlic, then season it well all over with salt and pepper.

Place the onions in a Dutch oven, pour half the wine over and lay the mutton on top. Use the remaining rosemary sprigs as a brush to coat the lamb with 2 tablespoons of the honey.

Cover with the pot's lid, place on the grill, close the EGG's lid and roast for 2½–3½ hours until the lamb is a deep brown colour and meltingly tender. As it is roasting, brush the meat occasionally with the remaining honey, and add a splash more wine if it is drying out.

Leave to rest for 20 minutes before serving.

EGG SET UP
Indirect set-up; convEGGtor in legs-up position with the stainless-steel grill on top of the convEGGtor legs. You'll need a Dutch oven.

TARGET TEMP
180–200°C/355–390°F

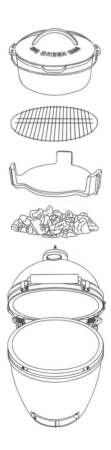

BAKING

The gift the EGG gives you when baking is enough heat. A conventional oven will never get hot enough to give you the 'oomph' you need to get that authentic crust or smoky hint of flavour on breads and pizzas.

You will notice in this chapter that some of the recipes require direct and indirect set-ups. The thinner breads will take the direct heat and cook quickly. The recipes that need cooking through, or the thicker breads, will need an indirect set-up. Double check before you start to cook. And when using a baking stone, give the EGG a little longer to heat up, and make sure you preheat the stone, so that what you are cooking doesn't stick.

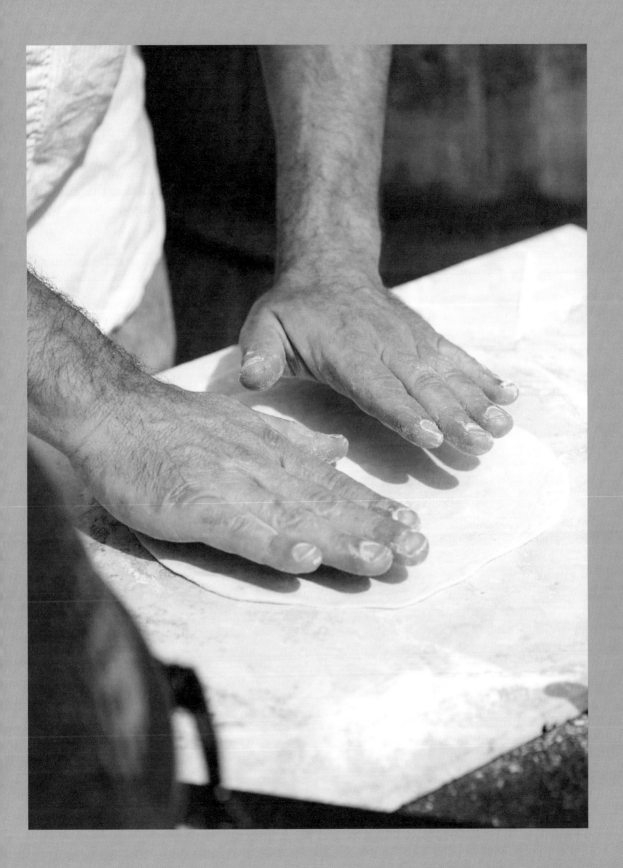

JALAPEÑO & SOUR CREAM CORNBREAD

SERVES 6–8

EGG SET UP
Direct set-up with baking stone on top of the stainless-steel grill. You'll need a skillet.

TARGET TEMP
170–200°C / 340–390°F

Cornbread is the classic Deep South BBQ side. It's worth mastering because it sits so well beside BBQ pork and beef, and I love it when it's still foaming butter and bubbling honey when it comes to the table... Use a skillet or metal baking dish about 20cm/8in across.

200g/1⅓ cups coarse cornmeal (or polenta)

100g/scant ½ cup sour cream

150ml/⅝ cup buttermilk

1 tbsp vegetable oil

1 tbsp honey or brown sugar

2 eggs, beaten

50g/½ packed cup grated Cheddar, or use another good cooking cheese

2–4 fresh jalapeño chillies, finely chopped (deseeded if you want less heat)

1 tbsp dried oregano (preferably Mexican)

1 tsp salt

1 tsp baking powder

¼ tsp bicarbonate of soda (baking soda)

50g/3½ tbsp butter

Toast the cornmeal in a dry skillet or baking dish in the EGG for a few minutes until toasted and fragrant.

In a bowl, mix together the toasted cornmeal with the sour cream, buttermilk, oil, honey or sugar, eggs, grated cheese, chopped chillies, oregano, salt, baking powder and bicarb.

Place the butter in the skillet or baking dish, place on the baking stone and leave for 3–5 minutes until it foams and begins to caramelize, turning nut brown without burning. Pour in the cornbread batter, close the lid and bake for 20–25 minutes until firm to the touch and golden brown, or until a skewer inserted into the middle comes out clean. Best served immediately.

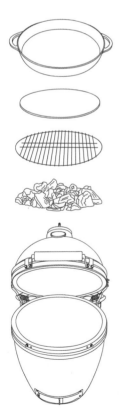

NAAN

Of all the things I've cooked in and on the EGG, nothing has given me greater pleasure than mastering naan. I mean it, and here's why... some things with a conventional oven are simply out of reach. Getting the bubbly top with leopard print burn and that mix of crisp and chewy texture in a naan is one of them. They make a curry for me, and now I am never without them or, even worse, having to eat disappointing ones.

I usually make double this recipe and freeze the ones that don't get eaten. Make sure you preheat the baking stone.

MAKES 4

EGG SET UP
Make the dough before lighting the EGG.

Direct set-up with baking stone on top of the stainless-steel grill.

TARGET TEMP
250–280°C / 480–535°F

130ml / scant ½ cup milk

2 tsp fast-action dried yeast

2 tsp sugar

300g / 2 cups plus 2 tbsp strong white bread flour, or 300g / 2¼ cups plain (all-purpose) flour, plus extra for dusting

1 tsp nigella seeds

1 tsp cumin seeds

100g / scant ½ cup plain yogurt

2 tbsp vegetable oil, plus extra for greasing

½ tsp salt

Softened butter or ghee, for brushing

Warm the milk until tepid and stir in the yeast and sugar. Stir this mixture into the flour with the nigella seeds, cumin seeds, yogurt, oil and salt to form a soft sticky dough. Cover and leave for 10 minutes, to allow the flour to soak up the liquid.

Knead for a couple of minutes to a smooth, soft dough, then place in an oiled bowl and allow to prove for 30–60 minutes, until doubled in size.

Divide the dough into 4 balls. Flatten one of the balls then roll it into an oval, about 20cm / 8in in length.

Transfer to the hot baking stone, close the lid and cook for 1–2 minutes until beginning to char in small patches and puff up, then flip over and cook on the other side for 1 minute. Place on a plate, cover with a clean cloth and repeat with the rest of the dough. Give each naan a little brush of butter or ghee before serving.

VARIATIONS

Quick Peshwari: Mix about 40g / 1½oz finely chopped raisins with 20g / ¾oz finely chopped pistachios or flaked (slivered) almonds, and use your thumb to push the mixture into the centre of the dough balls before rolling out. Dust the cooked naan with a pinch of garam masala.

Garlic: Fry 2 finely chopped garlic cloves in 25g / 1¾ tbsp butter for 30–60 seconds until aromatic. Drizzle the garlic butter all over the cooked naans instead of brushing them with butter or ghee.

PARATHA

The BBQ restaurant Temper in London is one of my favourite places to eat. They serve paratha with everything, which is a really good idea, so don't restrict these to just Indian or Asian dishes. I like to serve steak on them, sliced and fanned out. Make sure you preheat the baking stone.

500g / 3¾ cups plain (all-purpose) flour, plus extra for dusting

½ tsp sugar

1 tsp salt

300ml / 1¼ cups water

40g / 3 tbsp butter or ghee, melted

Mix the flour with the sugar and salt, then mix in the water to make a soft dough. Cover and put to one side for 5 minutes, then knead for a couple of minutes until smooth.

Separate the dough into 8 pieces and, on a floured surface, roll each piece into a circle about 15cm / 6in in diameter, then brush each with a little melted butter or ghee. Roll each up into a cigar shape, with the buttered side inside, then coil up the cigar into a snail. Press down with the palm of your hand and roll out again to a circle about 15cm / 6in in diameter.

Add to the hot baking stone, close the lid and cook for 1–2 minutes until beginning to char in small patches, then flip over and cook for the same time on the other side. Brush with a little butter or ghee (or do this just before serving) then place in a bowl and cover with a clean cloth while you repeat with the rest of the dough.

MAKES 8

EGG SET UP
Make the dough before lighting the EGG.

Direct set-up with baking stone on top of the stainless-steel grill.

TARGET TEMP
250–280°C / 480–535°F

LAHMACUN

When I first met my partner, Sushila, she lived in Finsbury Park, London. Our late-night fast-food go-to was a little kebab shop by the station that did lahmacun for a few quid. Loads of chilli sauce, loads of garlic sauce, then we wrapped them up and scoffed them down. This is a little more refined, but not much. Instead of the minced (ground) meat you could use up leftover cooked meat, finely chopped or shredded. Make sure you preheat the baking stone.

MAKES 4

EGG SET UP
Make the dough before lighting the EGG.

Direct set-up with baking stone on top of the stainless-steel grill.

TARGET TEMP
250–300°C / 480–570°F

For the dough
500g / 3½ cups strong white bread flour, plus extra for dusting

1 tsp fast-action dried yeast

1 tsp salt

300ml / 1¼ cups water

Olive oil, for oiling your hands

For the topping
150g / 5¼oz minced (ground) lamb, goat or beef

1 tbsp tomato purée (paste)

1 tsp ground coriander

Large pinch of ground cinnamon

1 tsp ground cumin

1 tsp dried chilli flakes (preferably Turkish)

1 tsp salt

2 tbsp olive oil

½ green or red (bell) pepper, deseeded and very finely chopped

1 small onion, very finely chopped

½ small bunch of flat-leaf parsley, leaves picked

4 tomatoes, sliced

1 lemon, cut into wedges

For the dough, put the flour, yeast and salt in a big mixing bowl, and mix in the water using a spoon, until combined completely. Place a damp cloth over the bowl and leave for an hour or so until almost doubled in size.

Mix the minced meat, tomato purée, spices, salt, olive oil and chopped pepper and onion, and put to one side.

Turn the dough out onto a lightly floured surface and knead it gently, with lightly oiled hands, for a couple of minutes. Cut the dough into 4 and, on a well-floured surface roll each ball into a thin oval shape, about 40cm / 16in in length, getting the dough as thin as possible without tearing.

Lay the lahmacun on the hot baking stone and spread a quarter of the topping all over the dough. Close the lid and bake for 6–8 minutes until the dough is crisp and the topping is cooked, then repeat with the remaining dough and topping. Serve immediately topped with the parsley and sliced tomato, and with the lemon wedges for squeezing.

BLACK PUDDING, POTATO & FENNEL TART

I am a chef of a certain vintage – the St. John vintage, and there are a lot of us. Chefs whose formative cooking years were shaped by Fergus Henderson and his now world-famous St. John restaurant. This tart feels like something you would see on the chalkboard next to the bakery section before heading upstairs for an excellent lunch.

100g / 3½oz small waxy potatoes

30g / 2 tbsp butter

2 large shallots or small red onions, thinly sliced

1 small fennel bulb, trimmed and very thinly sliced

350g / 12¼oz flaky or puff pastry (shop-bought is fine)

50g / scant ¼ cup crème fraîche

400g / 14oz black pudding (blood sausage), boudin noir or morcilla, cut into thin slices

Small bunch of flat-leaf parsley, leaves roughly chopped

Salt and freshly ground black pepper

Cook the potatoes in boiling, salted water on the stove for 15 minutes until just tender, then drain and, when cool enough to handle, cut into thin slices. Mix the butter through the slices to coat, season with salt and pepper, then mix with the sliced shallot or red onion, and fennel.

Roll out the pastry to a 25cm / 10in circle and place in the middle of the baking stone (at this stage unheated, and not inside the EGG). Season the crème fraîche with a little salt and black pepper, then spread it over the pastry. Scatter over the fennel mixture, then top with the black pudding slices.

Place the stone on top of the grill, close the lid and bake for 20–25 minutes until the pastry is golden brown and cooked through. Serve topped with the chopped parsley and another grind of black pepper.

EGG SET UP
Make the pastry before lighting the EGG.

Indirect set-up; convEGGtor in legs-up position with the stainless-steel grill on top of the convEGGtor legs; Baking stone to one side.

TARGET TEMP
150–180°C / 300–355°F

Make the filling before lighting the EGG.

Indirect set-up; convEGGtor in legs-up position with the stainless-steel grill on top of the legs, with baking stone on the stainless-steel grill.

TARGET TEMP
150–180°C / 300–355°F

ORANGE BLOSSOM HONEY & PISTACHIO PASTILLA

Folding over the filo pastry is a tremendously satisfying thing to do, but it is fiddly. Pastilla are extremely versatile and will hoover up almost any leftovers: chicken, lamb and goat are favourites, but roasted vegetables also work.

1 tbsp olive oil

2 onions, roughly chopped

3 garlic cloves, finely chopped

2 tsp ras el hanout

Pinch of saffron strands (optional)

1 tsp ground cinnamon

500g/1lb 2oz leftover cooked meat, finely chopped (or vegetables)

100ml/generous ⅓ cup chicken stock (or use water)

50g/1¾oz dried dates, apricots or raisins, roughly chopped

1 tbsp orange blossom honey (or use another floral honey), plus extra to serve

50g/1¾oz chopped pistachios (or use almonds)

3 eggs, beaten

Small bunch of flat-leaf parsley or coriander (cilantro), leaves finely chopped

5 large sheets of filo (phyllo) pastry

80g/⅓ cup butter, melted

1 tbsp icing sugar (confectioners' sugar)

Salt and freshly ground black pepper

Heat the oil in a pan on the stove, add the onions and fry for about 10 minutes or until soft and beginning to brown. Add the garlic, ras el hanout, saffron if using, and half the cinnamon, and fry for 1 minute more.

Add the meat and stock and season with salt and pepper to taste, then cover and simmer for about 10 minutes or until the meat is piping hot. Add the dried fruit, honey and nuts, then add the eggs and gently cook until the mixture just starts to resemble scrambled eggs. Add the herbs and put to one side.

Take a sheet of filo pastry and brush it with a little melted butter. Drape it over a baking dish or cake tin (pan), gently pushing it into the edges. Repeat with another sheet of filo, this time placing it at a right angle to the first. Repeat with the next 2 sheets of filo to form a large pastry case with no tears.

Spoon the meat mixture into the centre of the pastry, then wrap the pastry edges over the meat to make a pie. Lay the final sheet on top, brush with butter and tuck in any corners.

Place the dish on the hot baking stone, close the lid and cook for about 25–30 minutes until the pastry is a crisp and golden brown. Remove and allow to cool a little before sifting over the icing sugar and the rest of the cinnamon. Drizzle with a bit more honey to serve.

TLAYUDA

Tlayuda is an Oaxacan dish a little like pizza, but instead of a bread dough base it's a tortilla one. This is a great way of using up leftovers, and you can use more or less of whatever you have. You can use shop-bought wheat tortillas if you want, but I think making the tortillas yourself, with masa flour, is always worth the effort – press the tortilla out to the size of a side plate. A pizza paddle might come in handy for scooping them up.

SERVES 4

EGG SET UP
Make the pastry before lighting the EGG.

Indirect set-up; convEGGtor in legs-up position with the stainless-steel grill on top of the legs, with baking stone on the stainless-steel grill.

TARGET TEMP
180–220°C / 355–430°F

2 tbsp vegetable oil, plus extra for brushing

1 onion, finely chopped

4 garlic cloves, finely chopped

1 tsp toasted cracked cumin seeds

1–2 tsp chipotle paste or smoked paprika (to taste)

1 tsp dried Mexican oregano (or normal oregano)

1 x 400g / 14oz can of black (turtle) beans or kidney beans, drained (or 250g / 9oz cooked)

100ml / generous ⅓ cup water

4 large corn tortillas (see opposite for homemade)

500g / 1lb 2oz leftover roasted vegetables, roughly chopped (you can use meat too if you have it)

Salt and freshly ground black pepper

To serve

Charred salsa (page 188)

Quick pickled red onions (page 182)

200g / 7oz feta, crumbled

Small bunch of coriander (cilantro), roughly chopped

1 lime, cut into wedges

150g / ¾ cup sour cream

Hot sauce (optional)

Heat the oil in a pan on the stove and fry the onion and garlic for 5 minutes until soft, then add the spices and oregano and cook for 30 seconds until fragrant. Add the black beans and water, and cook for 5 minutes until rich and thick. Season to taste with salt and pepper and mash or blend to a coarse purée. Put to one side.

Brush the tortillas with a little oil, place on the hot baking stone one at a time, close the lid and bake for 1–2 minutes or until the bottom browns in patches. Place to one side, cooked side up, while you bake the others.

Smear the cooked side of each tortilla with the bean purée and top with the chopped vegetables. Place back in the EGG, close the lid and bake until the base is browned in patches and the topping is warm, about 3 minutes.

Serve as they come out of the EGG, topped with charred salsa, pickled onions, feta and coriander, with the lime wedges, sour cream and hot sauce on the side.

MASA HARINA SOFT TORTILLAS
(for tacos)

It is worth investing in a tortilla press. They're inexpensive and really make a difference. It's also a great way to get the kids involved. Make sure you preheat the baking stone or plancha.

250g/2 cups masa harina, plus a bit extra if needed

Pinch of salt

300ml/1¼ cups tepid water, plus a bit extra if needed

Mix the masa harina and salt in a bowl, add the water and mix until a dough forms and you can shape it into a ball, then knead a few times with your hands. Allow to rest for 10 minutes to see how the water is absorbed; you might need to add a touch more water or masa harina.

Divide the dough into 15–20 pieces and roll each into a ball, about the size of a ping-pong ball. Place a dough ball between two pieces of thin plastic or baking parchment and use a tortilla press, plate or heavy pan to flatten the ball into a circle. (You can use a rolling pin, but it might fray a bit at the edges.) Carefully peel off the plastic or parchment and repeat with the remaining dough balls.

Add one piece of flattened dough to the hot baking stone or plancha in the EGG, close the lid and cook for about 1 minute until just beginning to colour, then flip and cook for another minute. Remove and keep under a clean cloth to keep soft while you cook the rest.

Best served fresh. Alternatively, you can cool, cut into wedges and bake to make homemade tortilla chips.

MAKES 15–20 SMALL TORTILLAS

EGG SET UP
Direct set-up with baking stone or plancha on top of the stainless-steel grill (these can also be cooked directly on the grill – especially good if you have a cast-iron grid).

TARGET TEMP
250–280°C/480–535°F

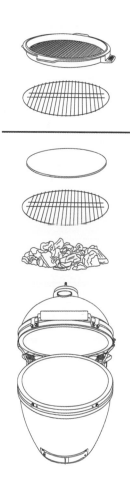

SAUCES AND CONDIMENTS

What you choose to cook on the EGG can be enhanced and modified by many sauces, pickles, chutneys, sprinkles or dips. Within this chapter are those I turn to time and time again in my cooking.

Those that are integral to the outcome of a recipe instead sit on the page of the recipe itself. Find them on the following pages:

Membrillo Alioli	page 64
Nam Jim Jaew	page 83
Satay	page 81
Romesco	page 91
Fennel Dressing	page 96
Ancho Dressing	page 106
Vinaigrette	page 109
Tamarind Glaze	page 135

MANGO KETCHUP

You can add a bit, or a lot, of chilli here if you like (either fresh or dried flakes), along with the other spices. If you can find, or make your own, fermented chillies, they give this sauce another layer. Thanks to my friend Sam Metcalf – who has a habit of leaving delicious gifts on my doorstep – for the inspiration here.

MAKES 2 SMALL JARS

1 tbsp oil
1 onion, finely chopped
400g / 14oz ripe mango flesh

100ml / generous ⅓ cup water
½ tsp ground allspice
½ tsp ground cinnamon
½ tsp ground ginger

¼ tsp ground nutmeg
½ tsp ground turmeric
60ml / ¼ cup cider vinegar
or white wine vinegar
Salt

Heat the oil in a pan and fry the onion for 5 minutes or until soft and translucent.

Add the mango to a food processor or blender, with the softened onions, water, spices, vinegar and a big pinch of salt, and process until smooth.

Return the mixture to the pan and cook for 10 minutes or until all the liquid has evaporated and you're left with a thick sticky sauce. Check the seasoning, then decant into sterilized jars.

QUICK PICKLED RED ONIONS

These go really well in so many dishes, including the goat raan on page 58 and the tlayuda on page 178.

**MAKES ENOUGH FOR
ABOUT 4 SERVINGS**

2 small red onions, thinly sliced
Juice of 2 limes or 1 lemon
Couple of pinches of salt

Plunge the onion slices into a pan of boiling water and boil for 1 minute, then rinse and drain well and place in a small dish. Squeeze over the lime or lemon juice and sprinkle over the salt. Put to one side for at least 30 minutes; they will keep for a week in the fridge.

TAHINI SAUCE

Great with the baked beetroot on page 151.

MAKES ABOUT 150ML / ⅝ CUP

½ garlic clove, crushed to a smooth paste with a pinch of salt

50g/3 tbsp tahini (sesame paste)

1 tbsp extra-virgin olive oil

Juice of ½ lemon

100ml/generous ⅓ cup water

Salt and freshly ground black pepper

Combine the garlic, tahini and oil in a small bowl. Add the lemon juice and whisk in the water a spoonful at a time, stirring briskly between additions to make a smooth sauce. The consistency should be like double (heavy) cream. Season with salt and pepper to taste. This keeps in the fridge for up to a week.

ROASTED GARLIC ALIOLI

You can use crushed fresh garlic, about 2–3 cloves crushed to a paste, instead of roasting it. Alternatively, omit the garlic for a plain mayo that you can flavour with whatever you like.

MAKES JUST OVER 400ML / 1⅔ CUPS
(or enough for 12 servings)

1 large head of garlic

2 large, free-range egg yolks

400ml/1⅔ cups sunflower oil (or use one-quarter extra-virgin olive oil and three-quarters sunflower oil)

White wine vinegar or cider vinegar, to taste

Salt and coarsely ground black pepper

Preheat the oven or EGG to about 180°C/350°F and roast the garlic bulb whole for 20–30 minutes until soft and sweet, then squeeze the flesh out.

Whisk the egg yolks with a big pinch of salt, a little black pepper and the garlic in a bowl. Put the oil in a jug that is easy to pour from, and slowly start whisking a few drops of oil into the egg mixture. Slowly increase the quantity of oil added each time, whisking in each addition so it is properly amalgamated, before adding the next. Once the mayonnaise has started to hold its shape you can start to add the oil in a thin stream.

When you have added all the oil, you should have a thick and wobbly mayonnaise that holds its shape. Taste and check the seasoning and add a dash of vinegar, salt and a generous amount of freshly, and coarsely, ground black pepper. It should be highly seasoned. It will keep for up to 3 days in the fridge.

HARISSA

It's worth making your own harissa; it has a much punchier and fresher flavour than shop-bought.

MAKES ABOUT 250ML / 1 CUP

1 red (bell) pepper, halved and deseeded

200g/7oz long red chillies

2 ripe tomatoes

50ml/3½ tbsp extra-virgin olive oil, plus a drizzle to seal

3 garlic cloves

2 tsp lightly toasted ground cumin

1 tsp caraway seeds

1 tsp sweet mild paprika

1 tbsp red wine vinegar

Salt and freshly ground black pepper

Roast the pepper, chillies and tomatoes on the grill in the EGG (at 200°C/390°F) for about 10 minutes until blistered and softened, turning all of them halfway through. Remove all the skins, and remove the stems and most of the seeds from the chillies.

Blend in a food processor or blender with the remaining ingredients to make a smooth sauce, adding salt and pepper to taste. Keep in the fridge topped with a layer of olive oil, for up to 2 weeks.

CUCUMBER & RADISH SALAD

More of a palate-cleansing condiment than a salad.

SERVES 4

1 cucumber, peeled and thinly sliced

300g/10½oz radishes, thinly sliced

Juice of ½ lemon or 1 lime, or vinegar, to taste

Pinch of salt

Pinch of sugar

Mix all the ingredients together and leave for 30 minutes before serving.

MINT RAITA

Other raitas can be made with dried mint, toasted mustard seeds or finely chopped chilli. Serve with whatever you fancy, to add a cooling element to any dish.

**MAKES ENOUGH FOR
12 SERVINGS**

10 mint leaves
250g/1 cup plus 2 tbsp plain yogurt
Juice of ½ lemon

Pinch of ground green cardamom (optional)
Pinch of salt

In a food processor or blender, blend together the mint, yogurt, lemon juice, cardamom, if using, and salt. Spoon into a bowl and serve.

DUKKA

Serve at the table to sprinkle over dishes, or even to coat food before roasting or grilling.

MAKES ABOUT 150G / 5¼OZ

75g/½ cup blanched almonds or hazelnuts
75g/½ cup sesame seeds
3 tbsp coriander seeds

1 tbsp cumin seeds
Salt and freshly ground black pepper

Toast all the nuts and seeds together in a hot, dry frying pan until fragrant. Tip onto a plate, leave to cool, then coarsely grind with salt and pepper to taste, being generous with the pepper. Store in an airtight jar for up to 2 weeks.

CHARRED SALSA

Perfect with tlayuda (page 178).

**MAKES ABOUT 300ML /
1¼ CUPS**

6 ripe tomatoes

6 garlic cloves, unpeeled

1 red onion, peeled and quartered

Handful of coriander (cilantro) leaves,
roughly chopped

Lime juice, to taste

2 dried árbol or pequín chillies, or another
medium-hot chilli (you can also use fresh
chilli if you like), finely chopped

Salt and freshly ground black pepper

Roast the tomatoes and garlic cloves along with the onion quarters on the grill in the EGG (at 200–220°C/
390–430°F) for about 10 minutes, turning every now and then until blistered and charred. Remove the skins
from the tomatoes and garlic.

Finely chop the charred vegetables and season with salt and pepper. Mix in the coriander and add lime juice to
taste. Add the chopped dried chilli. Store in the fridge for up to a week.

PIPIRRANA

Good with oily fish, vegetables and chicken, or even on its own on grilled bread.

**MAKES 200ML /
GENEROUS ¾ CUP**

2 hard-boiled eggs, peeled and finely
chopped

1 shallot, very finely chopped

2 large ripe tomatoes, deseeded and
finely chopped

1 green (bell) pepper, very finely chopped

½ cucumber, peeled, deseeded and
finely chopped

2 tbsp white wine vinegar, plus extra
to taste

50ml/3½ tbsp extra-virgin olive oil,
plus extra to taste

Pinch of toasted ground cumin seeds
(optional)

Salt and freshly ground black pepper

Mix all the ingredients together, seasoning with salt, pepper and more oil and vinegar, to taste.

GREMOLATA

As well as being an essential component in osso buco (see the veal recipe on page 67), this also works with most pasta or chicken dishes, or whole fish.

SERVES 4

Finely grated zest of 1 lemon

1 garlic clove, very finely chopped

½ small bunch of flat-leaf parsley, leaves finely chopped

Sea salt and freshly ground black pepper

Mix all the ingredients together, adding salt and pepper to taste.

SALSA VERDE

A punchy flavoured topping for pretty much anything in the European cuisine spectrum. This can be made in a food processor, but cutting by hand is better. Chopped cornichons can be added too.

MAKES 12 SERVINGS

4 anchovy fillets, rinsed if packed in salt

2 garlic cloves, finely chopped

Large bunch of flat-leaf parsley, leaves picked

Small bunch of basil or mint (or a combination), leaves picked

2 tbsp salted capers, rinsed and roughly chopped

1 tbsp Dijon mustard

2 tbsp red wine vinegar or lemon juice

About 100ml / generous ⅓ cup good-quality extra-virgin olive oil

Freshly ground black pepper

Mash the anchovies and garlic together in a pestle and mortar, then gradually add the herbs and capers and pound to a rough paste. Alternatively, chop the herbs, anchovies, capers and garlic with a large knife, all together, on a big chopping board, then place in a bowl.

Stir in the mustard and vinegar or lemon juice, then slowly whisk in the oil until you achieve your desired consistency. Taste and add more vinegar or lemon juice if you like, with pepper to taste.

Store in a jar in the fridge, with a thin layer of oil on the top.

ZHUG

Zhug has as many variations as it has spellings, but I'm going with this combination for this Yemeni chutney. It can be used as a dip, marinade or even as a sandwich spread. You can use a food processor to make this, but if you do, use ground spices instead of the whole seeds.

MAKES 250ML / 1 CUP

Seeds of 4 green cardamom pods

1 tsp coriander seeds

½ tsp cumin seeds

6 garlic cloves, chopped

4–8 green chillies, deseeded (depending on your taste and heat of chillies) and roughly chopped

Small bunch of coriander (cilantro), leaves roughly chopped

Small bunch of flat-leaf parsley, leaves roughly chopped

4 tbsp olive oil

Salt and freshly ground black pepper

Crush all the seeds with a mortar and pestle, with a pinch of salt, then add the garlic and chillies and grind to a very coarse paste before adding the herbs. Add the oil gradually while continuing to grind, then season to taste.

Store in a jar in the fridge, with a thin layer of oil on the top, for up to 2 weeks.

CHIMICHURRI

This can be pulsed or ground to a coarse purée if you prefer, either in a blender or using a mortar and pestle.

MAKES 12 SERVINGS

4 tbsp red wine vinegar

½ tsp salt

2 garlic cloves, finely chopped

1 small shallot, finely chopped (or use ½ bunch of trimmed spring onions/scallions)

½ tsp dried chilli flakes, or more to taste

1 tsp good-quality dried oregano

Small bunch of flat-leaf parsley, leaves finely chopped

2 tbsp fresh oregano leaves (optional)

6 tbsp extra-virgin olive oil

Salt and freshly ground black pepper

In a bowl, mix together the vinegar, salt, garlic and shallots, then leave to one side for 10 minutes.

Stir in the remaining ingredients and allow the flavours to develop for an hour or so before serving. It will keep in the fridge for up to a week (but will discolour).

ANCHOVY BUTTER

This is delicious melted onto the steaks on pages 55 and 104.

MAKES ABOUT 150G / 5¼OZ

1 x 50g/1¾oz can of anchovy fillets, drained and finely chopped

100g/scant ½ cup unsalted butter, cubed and softened

1–2 tsp fresh thyme leaves, roughly chopped

Pinch of dried chilli flakes, to taste

Salt and coarsely ground black pepper

In a small bowl, beat the anchovies into the butter along with the thyme, chilli flakes, and some salt and pepper to taste.

Once completely combined, shape the anchovy butter into a sausage shape, wrap it in baking parchment, and keep in the fridge.

INDEX

A

afterburner and dirty cooking 102
  ash-cooked sausage with shallot, red wine, garlic & thyme 107
  burnt aubergine, miso & black sesame dip 111
  escalivada 108
  hispi cabbage with jalapeño buttermilk & ancho dressing 106
  leeks vinaigrette 109
  migas-stuffed whole onions 110
  scallops in shell with hazelnut & herb butter 114
  steak on coals 104
  triple tomato salad: slow roast, raw & dressing 115

alioli
  membrillo alioli 64
  roasted garlic alioli 80, 183

almonds
  burnt calçots & Romesco 91
  dukka 187
  goat shoulder pomegranate raan 58–60

ancho chillies
  jalapeño buttermilk & ancho dressing 106
  mole 162
  pork ribs with ancho & citrus marinade 130
  whole crown prince squash stuffed with pumpkin seeds & chillies 128

anchovies
  anchovy butter 191
  escalivada 108
  salsa verde 189

ash-cooking
  ash-cooked sausage with shallot, red wine, garlic & thyme 107
  escalivada 108
  leeks vinaigrette 109
  migas-stuffed whole onions 110

asparagus: verdura mista 90

aubergines (eggplant)
  burnt aubergine, miso & black sesame dip 111
  escalivada 108
  leftovers moussaka 149
  verdura mista 90

B

bacon: roasted partridge with 'nduja, sultanas & sweet Marsala 140

baking 168–79
  black pudding, potato & fennel tart 175
  jalapeño & sour cream cornbread 170
  lahmacun 174
  masa harina soft tortillas 179
  naan 171
  orange blossom honey & pistachio pastilla 176
  paratha 173
  tlayuda 178

basil
  salsa verde 189
  verdura mista 90

beans: kamameshi 166

beef 40–4
  brisket 75
  corn-fed cattle 40
  cuts 44
  featherblade carbonnade à la flamande 154
  fragrant Sichuan short ribs 71
  grass-fed cattle 40
  hanging 40
  Japanese Wagyu 40
  lahmacun 174
  leftovers moussaka 149
  quick grilled short ribs with chimichurri 87
  reverse sear steak picanha 132
  salting 40, 55
  seared onglet à l'échalote 88
  standing rib roast 68
  steak 55
  steak on coals 104

beer: featherblade carbonnade à la flamande 154

beetroot, baked whole 151

bhuna, lamb chop 160

Bhushan, Santi 160

Big Green EGG, lighting and using your 12–23

bird's-eye chillies: grilled squid with nam jim jaew 83

black beans (turtle beans)
  coconut & habanero black beans 156
  tlayuda 178

black pudding, potato & fennel tart 175

bone marrow: filled baked potatoes: roasted shallot, bone marrow & rosemary 146

bread
  burnt calçots & Romesco 91
  jalapeño & sour cream cornbread 170
  lahmacun 174
  migas-stuffed whole onions 110
  naan 171
  paratha 173

brick chicken thighs with harissa 98

brill, whole 78

brining 62
  brined chicken breast 62

brisket 75

butter
  anchovy butter 191
  butter-bath chicken with piri piri 138
  hazelnut & herb butter 114
  pepper butter 155

butter beans: paella with roasted garlic alioli 80

buttermilk
  jalapeño & sour cream cornbread 170
  jalapeño buttermilk & ancho dressing 106

C

cabbage: hispi cabbage with jalapeño buttermilk & ancho dressing 106

calçots & romesco, burnt 91

capers
  leeks vinaigrette 109
  mackerel with fennel dressing 96
  salsa verde 189

carrots
  Dutch oven bone-in veal shin

pasta 67
roast root soup with pepper butter 155
whole carrots with zhug 147

celeriac: roast root soup with pepper butter 155

charcoal 26–7

cheese
corn with kikos crumbs 148
filled baked potatoes: tartiflette 146
leftovers moussaka 149
pizza 56
smoked ricotta 99

chicken 45
brick chicken thighs with harissa 98
brined chicken breast 62
butter-bath chicken with piri piri 138
chicken wings 46
cuts 45
green tandoori chicken 84
kamameshi 166
paella with roasted garlic alioli 80
roast chicken 52

salting 40

chillies
green tandoori chicken 84
grilled squid with nam jim jaew 83
harissa 186
jalapeño & sour cream cornbread 170
jalapeño buttermilk & ancho dressing 106
lamb chop bhuna 160
mole 162
prawn satay 81
whole crown prince squash stuffed with pumpkin seeds & chillies 128
zhug 190
chimichurri 190
quick grilled short ribs or sliced pork belly with chimichurri 87

chorizo
migas-stuffed whole onions 110
paella with roasted garlic alioli 80

ciabatta bread
burnt calçots & Romesco 91
migas-stuffed whole onions 110

citrus fruit
grilled squid with nam jim jaew 83
pork ribs with ancho & citrus marinade 130
mackerel with fennel dressing 96

clams: paella with roasted garlic alioli 80

coals, cooking on 102
hispi cabbage with jalapeño buttermilk & ancho dressing 106
steak on coals 104
see also dirty and afterburner cooking
coconut milk
coconut & habanero black beans 156
prawn satay 81

condiments
anchovy butter 191
charred salsa 188
chimichurri 190
cucumber & radish salad 186
dukka 187
gremolata 189
harissa 186
mango ketchup 182
mint raita 187
pirirrana 188
quick pickled red onions 182
salsa verde 189
zhug 190

cooking, managing the 30–6

coriander (cilantro)
goat shoulder pomegranate raan 58–60
green tandoori chicken 84
jalapeño buttermilk & ancho dressing 106

corn tortillas: tlayuda 178

corn with kikos crumbs 148

cornbread, jalapeño & sour cream 170

courgettes (zucchini): verdura mista 90

crown prince squash: whole crown prince squash stuffed with pumpkin seeds & chillies 128

crustacea 45

cucumber
cucumber & radish salad 186
pirirrana 188

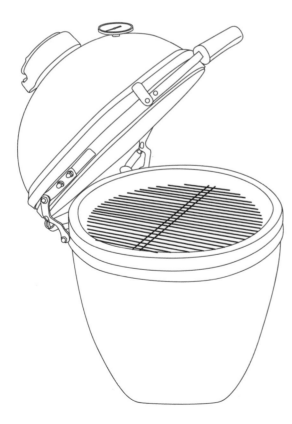

curry
    fish curry 163
    lamb chop bhuna 160
    Trini duck curry 158

D

dip, miso & black sesame 111

direct cooking 76–91

dirty and afterburner cooking 28,
    102–15
    ash-cooked sausage with shallot,
        red wine, garlic & thyme 107
    burnt aubergine, miso & black
        sesame dip 111
    escalivada 108
    hispi cabbage with jalapeño
        buttermilk & ancho dressing
        106
    leeks vinaigrette 109
    migas-stuffed whole onions 110
    scallops in shell with hazelnut &
        herb butter 114
    steak on coals 104
    triple tomato salad: slow roast,
        raw & dressing 115

dressings
    fennel dressing 96
    jalapeño buttermilk & ancho
        dressing 106

duck
    duck breast 94
    Trini duck curry 158

dukka 187

Dutch oven cooking 22, 152–67
    Dutch oven bone-in veal shin
        pasta 67

E

EGG, lighting and using your 12–23

eggs
    leeks vinaigrette 109
    pirirrana 188

equipment and tools 28–37

escalivada 108

F

featherblade carbonnade à la
    flamande 154

fennel
    black pudding, potato & fennel
        tart 175
    fish en papillote with Provence
        flavours 143
    mackerel with fennel dressing 96
    smoked mackerel 61
    verdura mista 90

filo pastry: orange blossom honey &
    pistachio pastilla 176

fire
    fire triangle 24, 26, 27
    managing the fire 28

fish 45
    anchovy butter 191
    escalivada 108
    fish curry 163
    fish en papillote with Provence
        flavours 143
    herbed side of salmon or sea
        trout 123
    mackerel with fennel dressing 96
    oily fish 45
    salsa verde 189
    salting 40
    smoked mackerel 61
    whole turbot 78

Fisher, Ed 9, 11, 48

flavour triangle 24, 27, 40

foil 71

food, holding the 36–7

fragrant Sichuan short ribs 71

Franklin, Aaron 50

fuel 26–7

G

garlic
    ash-cooked sausage with shallot,
        red wine, garlic & thyme 107
    burnt calçots & Romesco 91
    butter-bath chicken with piri piri
        138
    charred salsa 188
    Dutch oven bone-in veal shin
        pasta 67
    lamb chop bhuna 160
    migas-stuffed whole onions 110
    mole 162
    roast root soup with pepper
        butter 155
    roasted garlic alioli 80, 183
    zhug 190

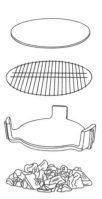

ginger: goat shoulder pomegranate
    raan 58–60

glazes
    spiced port glaze 123
    tamarind glaze 133

goat
    goat shoulder pomegranate raan
        58–60
    lahmacun 174
    leftovers moussaka 149
    whole roast kid 118

green (bell) pepper: double-cook
    lamb kebab with chopped salad &
    paratha 141

green tandoori chicken 84

gremolata 189

grilling see direct cooking

guajillo chillies: whole crown prince
    squash stuffed with pumpkin
    seeds & chillies 128

H

habanero chilli: coconut & habanero
    black beans 156

halloumi: leftovers moussaka 149

ham
    filled baked potatoes: tartiflette
        146
    whole ham with spiced port glaze
        124

hand tools 32–6

harissa 186
    brick chicken thighs with harissa
        98

hasselback potatoes, roast leg of

hogget crying over 144

hazelnuts
  dukka 187
  hazelnut & herb butter 114

Helou, Anissa 135

Henderson, Fergus 175

herbs
  hazelnut & herb butter 114
  herbed side of salmon or sea
    trout 123
  salsa verde 189
  zhug 190

hispi cabbage with jalapeño
  buttermilk & ancho dressing 106

hogget 45
  roast leg of hogget crying over
    hasselback potatoes 144

honey
  mutton shoulder with melting
    onions, rosemary & honey 167
  orange blossom honey & pistachio
    pastilla 176

I

Iberico pork 44

indirect cooking 136–51

ingredients 24, 40–5

J

jalapeño chillies
  jalapeño & sour cream cornbread
    170
  jalapeño buttermilk & ancho
    dressing 106

K

Kamado 9–10, 30

kamameshi 166

kebabs: double-cook lamb kebab
  with chopped salad & paratha 141

kecap manis: prawn satay 81

ketchup, mango 182

kid goat, whole roast 118

kidney beans: tlayuda 178

kikos crumbs, corn with 148

L

lacto-fermentation 40

lahmacun 174

lamb 44–5
  butterflied leg of lamb with
    moscatel & green olives 82
  cuts 44
  double-cook lamb kebab with
    chopped salad & paratha 141
  lahmacun 174
  lamb chop bhuna 160
  lamb rack with salsa verde 95
  lamb ribs with tamarind glaze 134
  leftovers moussaka 149
  prawn satay 81
  see also hogget; mutton

leeks
  burnt calçots & Romesco 91
  Dutch oven bone-in veal shin
    pasta 67
  leeks vinaigrette 109
  roast root soup with pepper
    butter 155

leftovers moussaka 149

lemons: mackerel with fennel
  dressing 96

lighting and using your EGG 12–23

limes
  grilled squid with nam jim jaew
    83
  pork ribs with ancho & citrus
    marinade 130

lobsters 45

low and slow 116–35

M

mackerel
  mackerel with fennel dressing 96
  smoked mackerel 61

mango ketchup 182

marinading and mopping 37

Marsala, roasted partridge with
  'nduja, sultanas & sweet 140

masa harina soft tortillas (for
  tacos) 179
  pork or ox cheeks with masa
    harina soft tortilla 121

meat
  orange blossom honey & pistachio

pastilla 176
  see also beef; lamb; pork, etc

membrillo alioli 64

migas-stuffed whole onions 110

mint raita 187

mise-en-place 37

miso: burnt aubergine, miso & black
  sesame dip 111

mole 162

mopping and marinading 37

morcilla sausages: migas-stuffed
  whole onions 110

muscatel: butterflied leg of lamb
  with moscatel & green olives 82

moussaka, leftovers 149

mozzarella: pizza 56

mussels 45
  paella with roasted garlic alioli 80

mutton 45
  leftovers moussaka 149
  mutton shoulder with melting
    onions, rosemary & honey 167

N

naan 171

nam jim jaew, grilled squid with 83

'nduja: roasted partridge with
  'nduja, sultanas & sweet Marsala
  140

O

olives, butterflied leg of lamb with
  moscatel & green 82

onglet: seared onglet à l'échalote
  88

onions
  migas-stuffed whole onions 110
  mutton shoulder with melting
    onions, rosemary & honey 167
  quick pickled red onions 182
  roast leg of hogget crying over
    hasselback potatoes 144

orange blossom honey & pistachio
  pastilla 176

oranges: pork ribs with ancho &

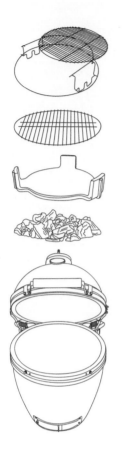

citrus marinade 130

osso buco: Dutch oven bone-in veal shin pasta 67

ox cheeks with masa harina soft tortilla 121

ox heart pinchos morunos 100

oysters 45

P

paella with roasted garlic alioli 80

paratha 173
   double-cook lamb kebab with chopped salad & paratha 141

parsley
   chimichurri 190
   gremolata 189
   mackerel with fennel dressing 96
   salsa verde 189

parsnips: roast root soup with pepper butter 155

partridge: roasted partridge with 'nduja, sultanas & sweet Marsala 140

pasilla chillies
   mole 162
   whole crown prince squash stuffed with pumpkin seeds & chillies 128

pasta, Dutch oven bone-in veal shin 67

pastilla, orange blossom honey & pistachio 176

peach paper 71

peanut butter: prawn satay 81

peas
   kamameshi 166
   paella with roasted garlic alioli 80

peppercorns: salt & pepper prawns 101

peppers (bell peppers)
   double-cook lamb kebab with chopped salad & paratha 141
   escalivada 108
   paella with roasted garlic alioli 80
   pepper butter 155
   verdura mista 90

picanha steak, reverse sear 132

pickled red onions, quick 182

pinchos morunos, ox heart 100

piri piri, butter-bath chicken with 138

pirirrana 188

pistachios: orange blossom honey & pistachio pastilla 176

pizza 56

plancha 23, 92–101

pomegranate: goat shoulder pomegranate raan 58–60

pork 44
   avoiding drying out 44
   cooking temperature 44
   cuts 44
   Iberico 44
   paella with roasted garlic alioli 80
   pork belly with membrillo alioli 64
   pork ribs with ancho & citrus marinade 130

pork shoulder with vindaloo spices 72
pork with masa harina soft tortilla 121
sliced pork belly with chimichurri 87
whole ham with spiced port glaze 124

port: whole ham with spiced port glaze 124

potatoes
   black pudding, potato & fennel tart 175
   filled baked potatoes: tartiflette or roasted shallot, bone marrow & rosemary 146
   pizza 56
   roast leg of hogget crying over hasselback potatoes 144

prawns (shrimp)
   fish en papillote with Provence flavours 143
   paella with roasted garlic alioli 80
   prawn satay 81
   salt & pepper prawns 101

puff pastry: black pudding, potato & fennel tart 175

pumpkin seeds: whole crown prince squash stuffed with pumpkin seeds & chillies 128

R

raan, pomegranate 58–60

radishes: cucumber & radish salad 186

raita, mint 187

red (bell) peppers
   burnt calçots & Romesco 91
   escalivada 108
   harissa 186
   paella with roasted garlic alioli 80
   verdura mista 90

red wine
   ash-cooked sausage with shallot, red wine, garlic & thyme 107
   seared onglet à l'échalote 88

redcurrant jelly: duck breast 94

reverse sear steak picanha 132

ribs
   fragrant Sichuan short ribs 71

lamb ribs with tamarind glaze 134
pork ribs with ancho & citrus
    marinade 130
quick grilled short ribs with
    chimichurri 87
standing rib roast 68

rice
grilled squid with nam jim jaew
    83
kamameshi 166
paella with roasted garlic alioli 80

ricotta
smoked ricotta 99
verdura mista 90

Romesco, burnt calçots & 91

root vegetables
roast root soup with pepper
    butter 155
see also carrots; potatoes, etc

rosemary
filled baked potatoes: roasted
    shallot, bone marrow &
    rosemary 146
mutton shoulder with melting
    onions, rosemary & honey 167
pizza 56
roast leg of hogget crying over
    hasselback potatoes 144

S

salads
cucumber & radish salad 186
double-cook lamb kebab with
    chopped salad & paratha 141
triple tomato salad: slow roast,
    raw & dressing 115

salmon, herbed side of 123

salsa, charred 188

salsa verde 189
lamb rack with salsa verde 95

salt
brining 62
salt & pepper prawns 101
salting beef 40, 55

satay, prawn 81

sauces and condiments 180–91
anchovy butter 191
charred salsa 188
chimichurri 190
cucumber & radish salad 186
dukka 187
gremolata 189

harissa 186
mango ketchup 182
membrillo alioli 64
mint raita 187
pipirrana 188
quick pickled red onions 182
roasted garlic alioli 80, 183
salsa verde 189
tahini sauce 183
zhug 190

sausages
ash-cooked sausage with shallot,
    red wine, garlic & thyme 107
migas-stuffed whole onions 110

scallops 45
scallops in shell with hazelnut &
    herb butter 114

sea trout, herbed side of 118

seafood 45
see also individual types of
    seafood

seasoning 40, 55

serving 37

sesame seeds
burnt aubergine, miso & black
    sesame dip 111
dukka 187

shallots
ash-cooked sausage with shallot,
    red wine, garlic & thyme 107
filled baked potatoes: roasted
    shallot, bone marrow &
    rosemary 146
seared onglet à l'échalote 88

shellfish 45

see also individual types of
    shellfish

Sichuan pepper
fragrant Sichuan short ribs 71
salt & pepper prawns 101

smoked ham: whole ham with
    spiced port glaze 124

smoked mackerel 61

smoked ricotta 99
verdura mista 90

snails: paella with roasted garlic
    alioli 80

soup: roast root soup with pepper
    butter 155

sour cream: jalapeño & sour cream
    cornbread 170

sourdough
burnt calçots & Romesco 91
migas-stuffed whole onions 110

spice blends
tandoori spice blend 60
vindaloo spice blend 72

spinach: coconut & habanero black
    beans 156

squash
roast root soup with pepper
    butter 155
verdura mista 90
whole crown prince squash
    stuffed with pumpkin seeds &
    chillies 128

squid
grilled squid with nam jim jaew
    83

paella with roasted garlic alioli 80

sriracha sauce: prawn satay 81

steak 55
  featherblade carbonnade à la
    flamande 154
  reverse sear steak picanha 132
  steak on coals 104

Stullard, Simon 114

sultanas (golden raisins): roasted
  partridge with 'nduja, sultanas &
  sweet Marsala 140

summer verdura mista 90

T

tahini sauce 183

tamarind: lamb chops with
  tamarind glaze 133

tandoori chicken, green 84

tandoori spice blend 60
  goat shoulder pomegranate raan
    58–60

tart, black pudding, potato & fennel
  175

tartiflette: filled baked potatoes 146

temperature 30–2

thermometers 30–2

thyme, ash-cooked sausage with
  shallot, red wine, garlic & 107

tlayuda 178

tomatoes
  charred salsa 188
  escalivada 108
  fish en papillote with Provence
    flavours 143
  leftovers moussaka 149
  pirirrana 188
  triple tomato salad: slow roast,
    raw & dressing 115

tools and equipment 30–39

tortillas
  masa harina soft tortillas 121, 179
  tlayuda 178

Trini duck curry 158

turbot, whole 78

Turner, Richard 55

V

Vandore-Mackay, Luke 56

veal: Dutch oven bone-in veal shin
  pasta 67

vegetables
  escalivada 108
  orange blossom honey & pistachio
    pastilla 176
  tlayuda 178
  verdura mista 90
  see also individual types of
    vegetable

vinaigrette, leeks 109

vindaloo spices, pork shoulder with
  72

W

wine
  ash-cooked sausage with shallot,
    red wine, garlic & thyme 107
  Dutch oven bone-in veal shin
    pasta 67
  seared onglet à l'échalote 88

winter verdura mista 90

wood 26

Y

yellow (bell) peppers: verdura mista
  90

yogurt
  double-cook lamb kebab with
    chopped salad & paratha 141
  goat shoulder pomegranate raan
    58–60
  lamb chop bhuna 160
  leftovers moussaka 149
  mint raita 187

Z

zhug 190
  whole carrots with zhug 147

JAMES WHETLOR

Winner of a James Beard award for his first book, *Goat*, James Whetlor of Cabrito Goat Meat worked as a chef for 12 years in London, before moving back to his hometown in Devon and working at River Cottage. His award-winning business, Cabrito, now sells goat meat to catering butchers and restaurants, from a network of farms across the country. *Goat* also won the Guild of Food Writers Best Single Subject Food Book of 2019.

BIG GREEN EGG

The Big Green Egg is the original and the best ceramic grill and oven, beloved by Michelin kitchens around the globe. Based on the Japanese kamado oven, the Big Green Egg includes NASA-specification ceramics and a design so sturdy that it carries a lifetime warranty.

The Big Green Egg lets the home cook create fantastic restaurant-quality meals to share with friends and family. Fuelled only by natural lump wood charcoal, it creates flavours and textures like no other, whether on the grill, oven roasting, smoking, 'dirty' grilling direct on the coals or cooking low and slow. The Big Green Egg is equally amazing for cooking poultry, meat, seafood and vegetables; check out more delicious recipes and tips at www.biggreenegg.co.uk.

ACKNOWLEDGEMENTS

Thank you to Sarah Lavelle. It's an enormous privilege to get to write a book, and you've let me do it twice. I don't think I'll ever be able to repay that debt. To the team at Quadrille for the help, support and design brilliance, with a special mention to Harriet Webster and Sally Somers for making editing enjoyable with their patience and good humour. Thank you.

To David Ezrine at Big Green Egg. Thank you. You've always been supportive, enthusiastic and generous with everything.

Thank you to Ross Anderson for his comprehensive lessons in Big Green Egg cooking.

I had so much help with researching this book. My experience has always been that people are generous with their time and knowledge. Everyone I spoke to was equally passionate about their subject and I always find that inspirational.

For the history of Japanese ovens and some wider background, I am grateful for the help of Dr Helen McNaughton at SOAS and Professor Simon Partner at Duke University. And thank you to Junya Yamaski for making it clear I didn't know anything and need to do more research. That is exactly the kind of help I need!

Thank you to Alex Pole, Joe Garnett and Steve House who spent the day showing and explaining the art of forging and tool making.

Phillip and Ian Warren were kind enough to show me the ropes of Cornish farming and to explain why what they do is so vital to the ecology and the economy of the area (and why their meat is so damn good).

Charcoal Matt and T-Bone Chops for making the best charcoal in the word and caring enough about forestry management and the wider environment to do it. Trail blazers.

To Matt, Claire, Grace, Ivy and Dot. All have, to varying degrees, had a hand in developing, tasting and critiquing. Thank you. No more goat for a while, Ivy. I promise.

To Luke, Sara, Murdo, Sula and Skye (and Huck, I guess) at High Grange. Thank you for letting us take over your beautiful house and generally disrupt your life for a week.

Thanks to Harry, Emily, Raffy and Alegra for letting us make friends with your cows and take some photos.

Sam Folan – I think the pictures in the book speak for themselves. Extraordinary work. Thank you for making it so easy.

Alohla Bonser-Shaw and Faye Wears for styling and making it all so pretty and delicious.

Thanks to Sytch Farm, Netherton Foundry, Hodmedods, Flying Fish, Trill Farm, Alex Pole, Cornish Sea Salt, Wild Beer and Warrens Butchers for all the bits and pieces that made the book look so good.

Thanks to Chyenne Smith at J Lazy S Ranch in Idaho for a peek into the right kind of US cattle farming.

Thanks to Mark, Marcus, Chris, Rob, John F, Clay, Jon R, Stu, Pete, Angela, Jon D, Nathan and Christine for all the help, advice and enthusiasm over the years, particularly when I started cooking outside. Pushers, the lot of you.

Finally, to Moles, Elwood and Mika. Thank you for being enthusiastic tasters and honest critics. I love you.

SUPPLIERS

Below are a few things I enjoy and use to improve my cooking, eating and general Big Green Egg experience:

Sytch Farm Pottery
Gill's hand-thrown pottery, made from Cornish clay, is exquisite.
The vibrant colours make the dining table look superb.
sytchfarmstudios.co.uk

Netherton Foundry
The Netherton kit is prefect for oven-to-table cooking. I love using it.
It makes cooking, prep and presentation so much easier.
netherton-foundry.co.uk

Cornish Sea Salt
Good food needs good salt. This might seem like the sort of thing that won't make much difference, but it does. The chilli one is a particular favourite in my house.
cornishseasalt.co.uk

Alex Pole Ironwork
Alex and his team hand forge everything you need to cook and eat around fire.
It has a functional beauty and heft in the hand that I just adore.
alexpoleironwork.com

Hodmedods
British pulses and grains that constantly have me thinking 'I can't believe they manage to grow that here...' but they do, you know.
hodmedods.co.uk

The Wild Beer Co
The wild beer team constantly coming up with new, interesting flavours and experimenting with brewing techniques. There is always something to complement whatever you are cooking or occasionally be an ingredient.
wildbeerco.com

Warrens Butcher and Grazers
Quite simply the best meat in the business. No fuss, no gimmicks. Just the best animals, reared in the best way, by small producers keeping a rural economy going.
philipwarrenbutchers.co.uk

Flying Fish Seafoods
Top quality and sustainably sourced seafood from Cornwall. Huge thanks to Johnny and his amazing team.
flyingfishseafoods.co.uk

The photoshoot for the book took place at the beautiful **High Grange, Devon.**
highgrangedevon.com

Big Green Egg
All Big Greens Eggs in the book generously supplied by Big Green Egg UK.
biggreenegg.co.uk

Publishing Director
Sarah Lavelle

Junior Commissioning Editor
Harriet Webster

Copy Editor
Sally Somers

Designer
Alicia House

Cover Design
Will Webb

Illustrator
Sarah Fisher

Photographer
Sam Folan

Food Stylists
James Whetlor
Matt Williamson
Alohla Bonser-Shaw

Prop Stylists
Faye Wears
Alohla Bonser-Shaw

Head of Production
Stephen Lang

Production Controller
Sinead Herring

First published in 2021 by Quadrille,
an imprint of Hardie Grant Publishing

Quadrille
52–54 Southwark Street
London SE1 1UN
quadrille.com

Text © James Whetlor 2021
Photography © Sam Folan 2021
Design and layout © Quadrille 2021

Images on pages 28–29, 33, 36–37, 44–45, 48–49 © BGE,
courtesy of Matt Austin, Ross Brind and With Love

Cataloguing in Publication Data: a catalogue record for
this book is available from the British Library.

ISBN: 978 1 78713 587 1

Reprinted in 2021
10 9 8 7 6 5 4 3 2

Printed in China